INCORRIGIBLY
PLURAL

Incorrigibly Plural

Fiction and Poetry from the M Phil in Creative Writing at the Oscar Wilde Centre, School of English, Trinity College, Dublin.

First published by Lemon Soap Press 2006
Copyright © Lemon Soap Press

Incorrigibly Plural gratefully acknowledges
the generous financial support of the School of English, TCD.

ISBN 0-954-7650-3-6

Cover design, text design and typesetting by Anú Design
Printed and bound by Colour Books Ltd, Dublin

Incorrigibly Plural
Oscar Wilde Centre for Irish Writing
21 Westland Row
School of English
Trinity College Dublin
Dublin 2
REPUBLIC OF IRELAND

For information on the M. Phil. in Creative Writing
visit www.tcd.ie/OWC
For information on other masters programmes offered by the School of English visit
www.tcd.ie/English/index.php
or for M. Phil. in Literary Translation visit
www.tcd.ie/Arts_Letters/translation/index.php

World is crazier and more of it than we think,
Incorrigibly plural. I peel and portion
A tangerine and spit the pips and feel
The drunkenness of things being various.

Louis MacNeice, *Snow*, 1935

Staff

Acknowledgements

Many thanks to Gerald Dawe, Deirdre Madden and Carlo Gébler for advice and feedback; Jonathan Williams and Emma Farrell for editorial and proofing; Sarah Binchy and John Durnin for production and editorial wisdom; Terry Foley and Karen Carty in Anú Design for visual inspiration and layout; Sharon Conway in ColourBooks for print management; Brenda Brooks; David Higham Associates Ltd, and the Louis MacNeice Estate for allowing us to use the words from Snow; *The Irish Times*, Dr Stephen Matterson and Trinity College, School of English. Extra thanks to Lilian Foley of the Oscar Wilde Centre for her incredible support and tireless response to queries, and finally to all who have helped and contributed towards this anthology.

Contents

Foreword

As the creative writing programme at the Oscar Wilde Centre, School of English, Trinity College Dublin approaches its tenth anniversary in 2007-08 it's good to see that the commitment of this year's group of students shows no sign of sitting back on the laurels of previous years. Since 1997, when Trinity became the first university in Ireland to offer a Masters degree in creative writing, the programme has attracted an extraordinary range of applicants from many parts of the world. With such widely diverse backgrounds, contrasts in age and experience, it is no wonder that the workshops and seminars, which take place in 21 Westland Row, prove to be lively, challenging and inspiring to all the students and faculty, resident and visiting writer fellows alike. A fitting collaborative, creative and critical atmosphere for the house in which Oscar Wilde was born.

With *Incorrigibly Plural*, the exclusive production of this year's writers, the M Phil students are responsible for all aspects of taking the book from production through to final editing, although as with previous years, the ongoing assistance of literary agent and editor, Jonathan Williams has been invaluable. In what follows, the Master of Philosophy students give an intriguing insight into where their work as individuals, and as a group, presently stands; a fascinating snapshot of work in progress; a view from the room in which all fourteen writers read, discussed, revised, revisited, recast, re-imagined, what they set out to do when they arrived here first, from various arts and parts, late last September, 2005. Now many months, many workshops and seminars later, *Incorrigibly Plural* is a marker along the road – the road ahead.

Eleven fiction writers, three poets: *Incorrigibly Plural* takes us from a stalled robbery in contemporary Dublin, to a fire escape in New York where the neighbourhood looked 'different one flight up'; from a checkout and notions, in a dormitory town in Ireland, to jolly ruminations of bygone days; from rain-soaked Cambodia, to swimming and apocalypse in the West of Ireland and America; from family life and sin Irish and Canadian style, to prose poems like 'Snow after Istanbul'. If the city is heaving against the back window, as one of the poems has it, throughout the terrain represented in *Incorrigibly Plural* there is a tremendous sense of open spaces, new territories, talking heads, private intimacies, discovered voices. Which is, I imagine, precisely what Louis MacNeice meant in his landmark poem, *Snow*, after which this book takes its title, about feeling the drunkenness of things being various.

Gerald Dawe
April 13th 2006

Closed due to Robbery

GERARD LEE

air play to Oxo, the sign was a touch of class. Nailer and Keogh had us convinced we'd need a shooter. Paudge Daly was on for a jump-over, in and out. Me, I fancied having a go at the delivery van, when they're exposed like. There was nearly killings over it.

We were in Keogh's gaff. His aul lad came in and all in the height of it, after Paudge flicked a wet towel in Nailer's face because Nailer said Paudge was a fat cunt and couldn't jump over his ma's mickey. There was some crack from the towel. Nailer hit the deck roarin' like the Garda were interviewin' him. It caught Nailer's lip lovely, he looked like he had a few lips after. At first you couldn't see properly with all the blood and all, but when it eased off a bit, it looked mad. Like Sonny Jordan's pit-bull had a go off him. We had a teacher in our old school who used to say 'don't give me any of your lip', and I thought about it, but I didn't say it. Keogh's aul lad is in loads of scraps and he didn't give a bollix, only he was tryin' to watch the match and wanted us to keep it down. So everyone kind of relaxed a bit after that. Well, everyone except Nailer.

Then eventually Oxo goes 'Well that changes the plan inanyway.' See Nailer was going to say 'give us the cash' to the aul geebag in the Post Office, and point the gun and all this. Not now with his lip like the hole on a scabby donkey.

So we had to go back to the drawin' board. I was glad because I didn't want nothin' to do with no gun. What if the fuckin' thing went off? And that's when Oxo comes up with his idea for the sign. He holds it up, and Paudge reads it out: 'Closed due to robbery', and then Paudge goes 'What's that Oxo, your homework for your fuckin' literacy class?' Even Nailer breaks his shite and the gash in his lip opens again and up goes another handful of bog roll.

I didn't get it at first either. I thought it was maybe because the aul one in the Post Office was a bit deaf or something, because Oxo's ma is old and a bit blind or whatever, and Oxo is always goin' on about being nice to lame people and old people and all the rest. By rights his ma should be well dead, because, apart from the fact that she's at least in her sixties, or fifty whatever, she's had about twenty heart attacks and she still smokes like a bleedin' exhaust pipe. You want to see her: one drag and the smoke is ash down to the filter. Put anyone off smokes for good watchin' her so it would. They should get her a job goin' around the schools, just get her to light up in front of all the young ones and young fellas. Tell ye, that'd sort them with the smokes. She worked in the markets all her life and she's still strong as a horse so she is. A bloke tried to rob her bag a while back on the quays and she knocked the bollix out of the poor cunt. He ended up in one of them neck brace yokes for about a year after. Got him off the gear though, having that fuckin' thing round his neck, because he used to be strung out all the time, but he couldn't score goin' around with a lump of scaffold bent round his neck, and now he drives a forklift. I heard she helped him get fixed up with the job and all, used her contacts. Felt sorry for him so she did. She says when she was young they were always poor but they managed somehow, because there was no drugs. I suppose the transport wasn't as good in the olden days, they couldn't get the stuff in or whatever. How she can remember that far back is what puzzles me though. Sure she knew anyhow he meant no harm in robbin' her. A mot and all now he has. Oxo's ma even gave this bird the once over before she'd let them out together. Makin' sure she was no junkie or whatever.

Inanyway Oxo has to explain to all the muppets, which is us all, because nobody's got a breeze what he's on about with this fuckin' sign of his. The idea is we just put up the sign in the window of the Post Office, and pull down the blinds when we're safely inside. Anyone wantin' to get in will read the sign, think the robbery's all over instead of actually still goin' on, and fuck off home and not stick in their big hairy nose. Sorted! No guns, no pole vaults over counters, no little old men who want to be heroes getting' their collar bones broken. Nice one, Oxo!

Keogh's little brother Greener has a stencil set that Santy gave him, so while we're all talkin' Keogh takes that and does a new sign out, real neat like. Then Keogh shows the new sign to Oxo, all proud and all. Oxo goes, 'What the fuck is that ye stupid pox? If *you* were being robbed, would you sit down with your crayons and draw a nice little sign? Go into the kitchen and make us a cup of tea, ye fuckin' pigeon, and let the rest of us get on with the job. Stencil me bollix!' That set Nailer off again. By this stage he has all dry blood with bits of jax roll stuck all round his mouth. Then new blood sprouts from somewhere, 'cause he's laughing again. I was thinking of sayin' he could be in what's it, Lord of the Rings, but then I didn't. But he reminded me of one of them creatures, a dork or whatever. We had a piss-break when Keogh made the tea, and then we planned the job properly. Fair enough Oxo talked the most, and he mostly told the rest of us to shut the fuck up if we said anything, but I still think he took our ideas on board.

So then after it was all agreed Paudge gets up and zips up his hoodie, pulls his baseball cap real low over his eyes, and pulls his hood down over it. Then he takes out his mobile and goes, 'OK, 15.35 hours, synchronise yezzer watches.' I looked over at Oxo, and he wasn't movin', so neither did I. Paudge looks at us all and goes 'Are yez right or wha'?' Even Keogh has this one sussed and he goes 'Are you goin' home for your tea Paudge?' Then Nailer sort of frowns and his hand goes for the jax roll on the couch beside him. 'One more joke and you'll need a fuckin' blood transfusion,' I said. But only in my mind. Nailer is an animal at the best of times, and I wouldn't risk it on a good day, but definitely not now, what with the lip and all. Then

Paudge smiles and goes, 'Look at yez, all big fuckin' talk a minute ago, but when it comes to doin' the deed you're like a bunch of aul ones. Is there one man among yez?' Then Oxo goes, 'Here boys, have yez heard Paudge's new album? Get Nicked or Die Laughin' Tryin'.'

Up goes the jax roll, tea slops all over the gaff, Keogh nearly chokes on a big gulp. I wasn't too sure what the joke was exactly, but when Oxo says something funny, normally I just laugh along and try to suss the joke after. So it turns out that the Post Office is closed for a half-day, and Oxo was plannin' for us to have a go the *next* day. I broke my shite then when I realised, and everyone's looking' at me goin' what the fuck? The joke was five minutes ago.

Next morning at half eight sharp Oxo rings us all, to make sure nobody was late for the robbery. Paudge was in the horrors because he had no time for breakfast, and arrives at the back of the flats with a roll and crips and a bottle of Coke. Then Keogh starts with all this, 'The Garda would like to speak to a big fat hungry pig from the flats about the robbery', and Oxo had to step in before there was another scrap. Then he done a final check on the plan with us all. The Post Office opens at ten every morning, so at a quarter-to I headed up that way with Keogh. Oxo went up with Paudge, because Oxo said he had to keep Paudge and Keogh separated. He said he'd have brought their mammies to mind them, only their mammies might not be on for them robbin' the Post Office. I'd say my ma would nearly give it a go though, because she says they're always leavin' her short on her book. On account of the state of his face, Nailer had to go up last, and on his own. I think the whole good was nearly gone out of it for poor Nailer over the lip.

The first part of the plan, the walk up to the Post Office, couldn't have gone any smoother. We all arrived more or less at the same time, but enough apart not to get the hairy noses out. Oxo even had us arrive from different directions, which I thought was a touch of class. We waited a few seconds for the nod from Oxo, and started to move in. Just as we get to the door, Keogh reaches into his pocket, and Oxo has a small freak attack and goes, 'What the fuck? I said no gun!' But Keogh takes out a letter and goes, 'I thought it would look more real, ye know, at a Post Office, to have something to post.' By the look on Oxo's face he was ready to abort, but then he sez, 'Yeah, grand Keogh, whatever, now let's do it.' I thought it was one of Keogh's better ideas myself.

So we slip in just as Mrs Post Office is reefin' her kacks out of her large cod-and-chips arse. Her mind is so much on that that she doesn't clock the four of us arrivin' all at once. Then after a few seconds Nailer comes in and nearly takes the fuckin' door off the bleedin' hinges because Keogh decides to stand right behind it, security or some fuckin' thing, fuck knows. Fact is he was supposed to be on Sellotape. At this point Two Ton Tessie releases her trunks and straightens up her big milk-bottle health board fuckin' magnifyin' glasses on the end of her little wart of a nose and has a scope at us all in her shop. Her eyes look like they're in a fish tank swimming around on their own. Her nose starts to go like the nose on the rabbit Nailer's little brother used to have. Keogh's da can do it too, make his nose go sort of in and out, like he's sniffin' something in the wind, a fart or whatever. I can sort of do it with my ears, move them like, but only when I'm on my own.

Inanyway Paudge decides to smile at her, which is a bad move. First off Paudge is a humpy cunt at the best of times, and he doesn't have very much experience at smilin', 'specially not at old grannies like Mrs Goldfish Bowl. At some young bird, maybe, if he was on for givin' her a lash, but not this bargain-basement waxwork. Second, Paudge only has a very few teeth left, after various misunderstandings with people over the years, and the survivors don't really look that much like teeth at all, more like bits of toffee sort of growin' out of his gums. Mrs Stamps licks her lips all nervous like and looks at Paudge. Paudge is tryin' hard to remember what people look like when they're being friendly, so he can do it. Twitch twitch goes her nose. While all this is goin' on, Keogh gets a bit excited and pulls the blind down on the door before Oxo gets the sign stuck up. The blind won't go back up for Oxo. When Mrs Fisheyes looks over to see what the fuckin' racket is, she sees Oxo under the blind, tryin' to get the sign up on the glass inside. Then she sees Paudge doing a Shane

McGowan. Then she sees mullet-mouth Nailer. Then she fills her kacks. That's what it smelled like inanyway.

There's a delay, like in the old western films Nailer's aul fella watches on Sunday afternoons, when they do all big shots of every-one's eyes, and nobody knows what's the story next exactly. Then Oxo comes out from under the blind and fucks everyone out of it because he can't find the poxy Sellotape to put up the sign. Nobody moves, but all the eyes, including the ones in the fish bowl, keep rolling around. Then out of nowhere Mrs O'Dea – because that's her name, my ma used to play bingo with her sister – goes for her gun. Only in this case it's not a gun, it's a phone, and nobody thinks she's ordering Chinese. Nailer puts his shoulder into the door that goes behind the counter, which Mrs O'Dea never had time to lock yet, so Nailer goes straight through the door and creases himself on a parcel to New York or someplace. At the same time two little old dears come in linkin' each others' arms, because Oxo has left the door to look for the Sellotape. Four more eyes join the party. Our Post Office is fairly small, and at this stage, with eight people in it, it's startin' to feel a bit cramped, and not really ideal for pullin' off a robbery. Then one of the zimmers clocks Keogh, and starts askin' after his sister Stacey, and his little brother Greener, and his Da, and his Ma and every other cunt. Then someone else pushes at the door, and Oxo puts his head out and says the place is packed, which is sort of true, because it is, and asks them to wait.

So it's now only six minutes past ten, and there's no plan B. At least Nailer pulled out the phone wire while he was lookin' for more tissues, because the New York delivery had opened up his lip worse than ever. Mrs MilkBottle meanwhile was left just standin' there the whole time, with the phone in her chubby little stamp-deliverin' paw, like she'd forgotten what a fuckin' phone was. The old dears got a shock when Nailer came back out, in fact so did I when I saw the state of him, but then they started with all this, 'Aah you poor lad, did you hurt yourself?' and all the rest of it. Then out of nowhere I goes, 'Yeah, he just leaned against that door, missus, because he's had the virus, the 'flu, 'flu virus, yeah, and he was a bit weak, ye know, the way ye would be, and next thing he fell through that door there, missus, because it wasn't locked, although he thought it was, so he did, didn't ye, yeah, and look at him now, missus. His poor face is all messed up bad. I wouldn't be at all surprised if he looked for some compensation out of all this, I mean what mot would want to kiss him now?'

By the time I'm finished, everyone, even Oxo, is lookin' at me. If I could've took my own eyes out, I would've been lookin' at me too, because I've no fuckin' idea whatsoever where it all came out of. Oxo is so moved he's left off watchin' the door again, and a few more pensioners are moochin' in at the back, delighted with a bit of action. Then, as if Oxo hadn't been shocked enough to discover brain activity in one of his followers, Keogh steps up, whips out his bogie letter, and goes, 'Yes, I saw the whole thing. I was here to post this get-well card to my old aunty in Cork, or wherever, and this bloke was clearly in rag order, or sick, or whatever, unwell, but he probably needed his giro to get medicine. Inanyway if he makes a claim against this Post Office, I'll be glad to act a witness.'

Someone called an ambulance on a mobile, and when it arrived nobody was sure whether it was for Nailer, Mrs Post Office or Oxo, because they all needed treatment. The Garda came and took statements from everyone, and some of the zimmers who weren't even in the shop said they saw the whole thing. They ended up with seventeen statements, all sayin' Nailer had sustained terrible injuries in a fall not of his own makin' at the Post Office. There's a whopper claim in, and Poker Face, Nailer's solicitor, says he's on to a winner, what with all the statements and all. Poker Face saw the CCTV tapes from the shop, but said it didn't look any way suspicious. 'Just a bit strange,' he said, 'the way everybody was just sort of standing there, staring', until Nailer fell through the door. Then it shows the aul dears coming in, and the statements cover the rest. Keogh had to tell the aul dears that his auntie in Cork, or wherever, died, because every time they saw Keogh they kept askin' him how she was. They even gave him a score to buy flowers for her grave.

The best part of it all though was after the Garda were finished takin' all the statements, and they both had a royal pain in their brown with the whole fuckin' thing. I just happened to look down as they were leavin', and there was this paper, stuck with bits of bandy Sellotape, and Nailer's blood, flappin' off one copper's big barge of a boot. And if you took out your eyes and held them close to this bit of paper on the copper's boot, you could just make out the words *closed* and *robbery*.

A Breath of Air

ANTONIA HART

Eleanor ate her peas. Some of the others in the dining room used their forks in their right hands, like spoons. Eleanor swept the peas across the plate with her knife and mashed them silently against her fork. She slid the peas off the fork with pursed lips.

The dining room was like a hotel dining room, but also like a school dining room. There were tables for two and four, menus and bud vases, but the tables were melamine-topped, the napkins rough tissue. Eleanor had never laid a table with a paper napkin. Everyone in the dining room was breathing out hot fishiness, and it was all Eleanor could smell. The man she sat opposite ate with his mouth open, dropping flakes of fish and lumps of mashed potato onto his cardigan and the backs of his hands. His head hung at an angle to his neck, so that he was looking right down into his own plate. Eleanor had seen him around. He couldn't lift his head any higher. She paired fork and knife, and laid them six to twelve on her plate. A pudding bowl, with a teaspoon jutting from it, waited in the spot where a wine glass might have sat. Eleanor ignored it.

Seventy-six. They can't make me. At seventy-six you have earned the right not to eat jelly.

She knew that much. She drank tea so strong she could feel it staining her teeth, from a cup so thick it sucked all the heat into itself.

'Come on.' The duty nurse was Barbara, and she cleared the teacups onto a trolley. 'You can finish your tea in the day room.' Barbara wheeled the half-drunk teas away.

'Why do they call it the day room?' Eleanor asked the man with the hanging head. He made a sound, and jerked his shoulders. Eleanor leaned over the table towards him. 'Why?'

He didn't rise from his slouch. Eleanor followed Barbara to the day room. She had to shuffle a bit to keep her slippers on. They didn't like you to wear your shoes indoors. Why, Eleanor couldn't say. Perhaps they marked the floors. Perhaps the nurses didn't like the idea of all that kneeling to buckle and lace, unbuckle and unlace, every morning and evening. There wasn't a fireplace in the day room, but there were six radiators, which were kept on, full blast, and the sofas and chairs which lined the walls were pushed up against them. Eleanor moved her hips back into the angle of a sofa. Her knees didn't reach the edge to bend, so her legs stuck straight out in front of her. The heat made her sleepy. If she were to nod off, she would prefer to be properly settled into the sofa; she'd seen more than one woman slide off to the floor in a doze, skirt and slip askew.

Barbara gave out the teas again.

This isn't my tea. I've never taken sugar. Why would anyone ladle sugar into their tea? Tea syrup. Disgusting.

There was no lipstick on the cup, but that wasn't to say there hadn't been one of the women drinking from it. Eleanor didn't touch the rim. There was a woman in this place who had a sort of chalky white paste at the corners of her mouth, small ropes of it drawn apart when she yawned, and Eleanor was afraid of it.

She set the cup and saucer on her thigh and let the tea go cold until Barbara came to clear it again. One of the nurses turned on the television. It was showing a football match. Someone in the corner turned on a radio, which had people phoning in for a quiz. Eleanor closed her eyes, which dimmed the noise.

Eleanor had a scene in her head. She was drinking fragrant Earl Grey, poured from a china pot through a silver strainer into one of

14

those lovely Minton cups. No, not Minton, they were something else, but there was a green-and-gold pattern around the rim. She knew the scene was real because of the cups. Anyone could daydream about a refreshing cup of tea, but no one could dream up those cups; they were the real thing and she'd owned them. Or she owned them.

If you had visitors, you got out of the day room. You could go and sit somewhere else with them, even if it was only in the reception area. At least it was cooler and quieter there. Eleanor had no visitors. Someone had come, before. It was hard to tell how long ago. It was hard to tell when someone would come again. She sat and listened to the cheers and roars of the football supporters in one ear, and the questions and answers on the radio in the other ear, for an hour and a half, until she was called for bed.

'Here's a lovely nightie,' Barbara said, laying it on the bed. It was smocked, with little leg of mutton sleeves and three pearl buttons at the V of the neck.

Pretty. Pearls.

Eleanor's parents had given her pearl drop earrings for her eighteenth birthday, and when she'd worn them at her party that night, they'd picked up the whites of her eyes, the gleam of her teeth, the sheen on her cheekbones. She still had some pearl studs, somewhere, but they outshone her yellowed eyes and teeth. Eleanor pulled her polo-necked sweater over her head, and unzipped her skirt. She pushed the skirt and slip down to her feet and stepped out of them. She was stiff today, so Barbara undid her bra from the back and helped Eleanor to slide the nightie over her head and shoulders. When the nightie covered her, Eleanor sat on the edge of the bed to roll down her tights.

Barbara was turning on the light in the bathroom.

'Teeth, loo, hands, face.'

She stood in the doorway watching.

Eleanor still found it difficult to use the lavatory in front of someone else, but Barbara always insisted on being there.

'Can't have you falling in or falling off now, can we,' she said.

Eleanor had never heard of anyone falling into a lavatory before, and if she were to fall off she would rather do it in private and then pull on the panic cord. She sat, and stared at the floor with the nightie bunched at her hips. The sound of urine trickling into the bowl echoed in the tiled bathroom. Barbara wanted to wipe her but Eleanor kept her knees closed and did it herself, so Barbara could neither reach nor see.

Keep away.

Bed lasted longer than the night. The light went off once you'd had the sheet tucked tight across your shoulders. Eleanor lay in the dark. She didn't feel tired, but there was nothing else to do at night except be in bed.

Bedtime. Still and warm. A book. Where are all those books? There were so many, on those shelves in my bedroom. Or the sitting room? A room that was mine, anyway. With books in it, the names on the backs, names on the spines, and sometimes I had to turn my head to read them. There was apple blossom on the road. That was spring.

Eleanor didn't see Barbara for some days. After supper and television one day, she came back, and brought Eleanor to bed in a different room.

'This isn't my room,' said Eleanor, running her palm down the white-painted door jamb.

'It is now. You were reallocated while I was away. Look, all your things are here.'

Someone had put a clock and lamp onto a table beside the bed.

'That's not my clock.'

Eleanor's clock had come with her, had always been with her. It was a foldaway travelling clock with Roman numerals on its square face.

'Of course it is,' said Barbara. 'Now. Bed.'

Eleanor took off her clothes and put on the nightdress she was given. It was long-sleeved and blue, tight across the chest, with trace scents of perfume.

The house was Victorian, redbrick, double-fronted, with the dry stems of a climber twining under the windowsills. Two shallow steps to the front door were sunken at the centre, like old mattresses. Eleanor used the stick they had handed her to get down the steps, then along the gravelled path. There were five of them on the walk, wrapped in scarves and hats and coats, so that Eleanor couldn't tell which people they were. The ferrule on the stick sank deep into the little stones, making steps and pressure hard to judge. She stumbled, and when she'd righted herself and looked up, she saw a young woman in a fitted tweed coat and a furry pink scarf, walking towards her and waving. Her name was Patricia. She came, sometimes.

Patricia kissed her. 'How are you?' She tucked a hand through Eleanor's arm. 'Do you want to finish your walk?'

Eleanor shook her head.

'No thank you. I'd like to talk to you. You're something to do with Eric, aren't you?'

'I'm his wife, so I'm your niece in a way, aren't I? Come on then, and we'll go in.' She patted her pocket. 'I've something here for you.'

When they were inside, a nurse brought them tea, and they sat on the sofa near the reception desk with the tea on a low table. Patricia pulled out a chocolate orange.

'Here you are – I brought you this. Have some with your tea.'

Eleanor took it, and picked at the box to open it.

Tea, tea, tea.

Her fingers didn't bend properly, and her misshapen knuckles seemed to point in odd directions. Her mother's engagement ruby slipped around on her wedding finger. No one had ever given her a ring to replace it. Fifty years or more that ruby had spent on her finger. They'd have to cut it off me now, she joked sometimes, but only to herself.

'How are things?'

Eleanor looked up from the chocolate orange.

'I don't like it here.'

'It's not that bad, is it? I mean, it seems pleasant enough. The nurses are all very nice.'

Eleanor split the orange into segments. She chose one, and pushed the others in their foil towards Patricia.

'I want to leave.'

'Aren't you happy?'

'No.' Eleanor put her hand on Patricia's arm. 'I'm not. They think I'm stupid. Or mad. You should see some of the others.'

Patricia had seen them – the woman who cast herself about onto sofas and tables; the other woman who refused to wash. Eleanor had never cast herself about, and liked to be clean.

Patricia bit her bottom lip and screwed up her eyes in a helpless way. 'I'm sorry you're not happy.'

'Why can't I leave then? Tell Eric I'd like to go home.'

Patricia stacked chocolate pieces on her knee. 'That's not possible,' she said. 'You know the house was sold.' She put her hands, warm and soft, over Eleanor's. 'We'd love you to come to us for a weekend, soon.'

Eleanor shook her head and slowly broke a segment of chocolate into tiny pieces. They had said that before, about the house being sold, but she knew it couldn't be true. They had said it before about the weekend, too. It didn't seem to fit together. At these times, when things were so complicated, it seemed to her as if someone had stolen all the words from her head and she had no way of counteracting what she was told.

My house and my life. My heart and my home. My eyes and my ears. There was a rhythm of phrases in her head. *My sticks and my stones.* No. That was nonsense. She changed the rhythm. *The heart of my life. My house is my home. The key to the door.*

She had no key, but she found she didn't need one. On the morning walk, through the garden washed by overnight rain, she trudged more slowly than the rest of the group, and found herself detached from it, facing the wooden gate in the wall. It was made of vertical planks, painted dark green, with a square lock and a round brass handle. The brass attracted her. Already burnished by palms, it looked cold, but ready to absorb the warmth of another hand. She touched it, grasped it, turned it, walked through the door and closed it.

Done. Out. Don't stop, don't ask. Act.

She stood on the wet grass verge of a country road. Her toes stung with the sudden freshness that seeped through her shoes. They had not given her a stick today, and she walked without help, walked until the narrow road widened, breathing through her scarf so that her breath surrounded her face, hot and damp.

I am walking. I am leaving. I'm going home.

Her shoes were sodden by the time the verge turned into a narrow strip of pavement, but she'd longed for this sensation of the wind teasing up her flattened hair and making her eyes water. The sense of the road ahead intoxicated her.

Possibility. When I come to a road I recognise, I'll get my bearings. If I walk for long enough, I'll come to where the china and the books are. The end of waiting all night for the breakfast bell. The end of having to look at other people.

There was gorse in the hedge beside her, tiny yellow flowers studding branches of glossy needles. The flowers were the strong yellow of daffodils, and when Eleanor crushed them between her blunt fingers, they released a coconut scent that made the inner corners of her jaw tingle. Behind the hedges were houses now, quite a few houses, so this wasn't proper country at all, but when she looked over the roofs and beyond the houses, she saw mountains, their rocky outlines softened by more clusters of the yellow gorse. Broom, they called it in some places, but in the Wicklow Mountains it was gorse, and if she had the mountains to her back, she was facing home.

Her feet squelched in her shoes, her thin nylon tights unable to absorb any of the water. The road was wider now than roads she knew, and bore leftward and downhill into a Y-shaped junction with a road on which cars drove at speed. A huge blue metal sign with white writing showed Wicklow to the left and Dublin to the right. The pavement ran out at the junction.

Stay behind the yellow line.

She turned right onto the road. She breathed in the sound and the shock of the cars that swept and hooted past her. What would it be like to travel at such speed? Invigorating. Eleanor longed to test the energy that surged within her. But her throat and lungs were tightening now and her breath was making a hiss as she breathed out. She leaned against a metal fence that bordered the road, and waited for her breathing to come evenly. The cold of the metal bar crept through the tweed of her coat and skirt into her hips. Perhaps the cold was not exhilarating, but menacing. It stiffened her hips and muffled other sensations so that she couldn't tell where her bones were, or even if she had any. There wasn't space to sit down on the tarmac, her legs would stick out into the road, and she wouldn't be able to bend her knees in time, if at all, to tuck them away from the cars and trucks that now sucked the breath from her mouth and rattled her against the metal barrier as they screamed past. She slumped a little, and let herself slide down the barrier.

I'll rest a little. See how I feel in a bit. Not sure I do have my bearings, now. Just sit for a bit.

Eleanor opens her eyes and orange lights flash in the night around her. She's cold, there are shrieks and gusts of speed, lights rushing past. People hold her upper arms and put a plastic cup to her lips. They lift her up and wrap her in a blanket. She is carried, put into a car, where it's warm. The doors are slammed. They are shut now and dull the road noises. A man starts the car and they drive off, slowly.

'You're all right, darling, you're all right.' A woman sitting beside Eleanor strokes her cold hands.

The car turns, and pulls into a gravelly drive. There are lamps ahead, and the redbrick house with the dead creepers twined under the windowsills. Inside there are people. They are waiting for her. Eleanor stiffens as the woman in a furry pink scarf approaches her, and when she half-turns away, a nurse in a pale blue dress and a white apron and cap steps forward and leads her away to bed. The nurse gives her a cup of tea, which Eleanor drinks in one mouthful, sitting on the edge of the high bed. The nurse wedges in two hot-water bottles, one for Eleanor's feet and one for her back, and tucks the sheet and blanket in tightly, so that Eleanor's arms are pinned. The heat from the hot-water bottles works through her body; the shivering stops. The nurse leans over her and Eleanor smells from her breath that she has eaten Marmite. Someone slips a spoon of something sticky between her teeth. She doesn't recognise the taste, but she lets it trickle down her throat.

Poems

THERESE CAHERTY

Nocturne

A man coughs in this foreign church,
air shivers, marble echoes
my father driving home.

The car is cold.
Beside him I twist for sleep
under his big black coat.

His smell flows gently
Sweet Afton, Cussons, Brylcreem, Bush.
His cigarette burns the dark.

He coughs, smokes, coughs
my lullaby.

The Dark

We drive into the eclipse.
It isn't dark, you say.

Sea feeds on the Wexford coast.
Soon the moon will dim the sun.

Warned of blindness,
we bend to the sand

where our shaded eyes find a stranded starfish.
Its five tarnished fingers span my hand.

Later we watch it slowly shrink
on the dashboard of the car.

I hear wonder in your voice
It isn't dark, you say again.

Yet I see rock and water
eat into the light around you.

Aoife

Some raise quivering fingers
and judge my act.

Only I know.

I slipped into his children's souls
and saw they yearned for water,
longed to climb the air,
thirsted for no one but each other.
They had this dream
and not another.

My act
was not a curse
for only I could feel
the depth of their desire.

And out of love and that alone
I gifted them and sprang them into swans, forever.

Landing

That area
between the stairs and bedroom
leads to sun – or moon,
is the point of transition,
not transformation;
site of exits and entrances,
a slipway between two worlds:
the landing strip.

Where the Lilac Grew

For a time this room belonged to the lodger
a fossil collector with a beard
whose eyes feasted on stone.

He left and then this room of polished surfaces was mine.
Its bed sagged lovingly in the middle.
Once, my mother sat with me through the night

writing furtive letters to that other man
who had strayed into hostile territory.
He stared wide-eyed from the picture on the dresser

and she said over and over, like a prayer
he will come back to us,
he will come back.

But soon his memory flattened
and streamed under the door
out into the garden, where the lilac grew.

Compass and blackbird

You took the wrong turn, he says,
but you can't go back. It's all one-way, now.

He leans a dirty hand on the car window,
so certain of himself, so near.

The compass needle dances on the dashboard
searching for direction.

He stares at the tarmac, remembering out loud
those other days when one road

would get you there and back.
In the distance, a blackbird taps for worms.

A Pale Horse

CRAIG CAULFIELD

There's that cold frosty one for y'all. Here now, I'll pop that there for ya. Sure is good to see ya after all these years, boy oh boy. Been way too long, brother. Now sit back, and I'll tell y'all what's been a-goin' on 'round here lately. Looky here. There's a photograph of Pinky. Now, Pinky is a sweetheart, mind ya, but she sure is one dern ugly ol' girl. Looks like a yellow-eyed dog for chrissakes. Reminds me of my fifth wife – with them beady eyes and toxic halitosis. Only thing was my fifth wife didn't have as much hair on her back as Pinky does. Had the same big, fat, pink ass though. But I'm getting ahead of myself. Now if you look over yonder at this here spread of mine – well, it was a spread till the last divorce, when I had to sell a hundred acres to a developer to get that alligator I was married to off my back – give her a fuckin' divorce settlement so she could run off to Nevada with that barrel-assed loser of an assistant manager who worked down the Quickie-Freeze. Sweet Jesus above. My Pappy's probably still a-spinnin' in his grave so hard he plum tore out of it. I reckon he's about to China by now after I'm a-sellin' off most of the family farm. God rest his soul. But I been retired now two years, and was down a bit on funds for that nut-grinder's settlement. Whoa, boy, breathe that fresh Florida air there. Woo-ee! Now, the day old alligator packed her bags was the happiest fuckin' day of my life, I'm a-tellin' ya. Freedom! Boy, I sure loves women, but I've had my fill of what goes on above the neckline of that species. Been alone ever since. Not all alone like some kind of a nutcase hermit, I got me my friends, but there's been no females in my life 'cept those sweet little honeys down at Hooters, and of course those nice little Oriental girls over at the massage parlor off the Interstate. So, Alligator runs off to Reno with lard ass Quickie-Freeze, and a seven-hundred-fifty-thousand dollar divorce settlement from yours truly, and I'm out here on the back patio one day just enjoyin' a brew and the breeze a-blowin' in off the Gulf, when the trucks roll in. Fuck me blind. I was assured that no account developer would put up a golf course like he promised, but shit no. No, no, no, brother. A year later I'm a-settin' right here lookin' at a fuckin' instant suburb. Now, not fifteen years ago there was barely any congestion in this part of the Panhandle. Apalachicola's always been sort of out of the way, south as it is of Tallahassee and Panama City. A fella could have some stretchin' room 'round these parts in years past. Now it's gettin' to be one sprawlin' mini-mall and housing development after another. They call that progress 'round here, y'know? So anyways, all these walls and fences shot up 'round the new houses they's a-buildin' and that was fine with me after a while. Eventually a fella can get used to anythin'. I got me a few dogs and chickens, and don't want 'em gettin' run over now with all the increase in traffic. Didn't have to pay a penny of my own to get my last two acres surrounded by a fence. Though I guess you could argue I paid seven-hundred-and-fifty big ones for it! Now, most of the people a-movin' into these big ol' McMansions a-sproutin' up all around like dandelions hereabouts is regular folks; some's yuppies with kids, some's retirees, some's snowbirds down from up in Yankee-land only in the winter months. But them people who moved in next door – holy smokes! It all started when they put that up. See that big ol' cross over yonder? I mean, Christ himself would have been impressed a-hangin' off o' that one. I think it's made out of fuckin' mahogany. Now, turns out these folks next door is from one of them fundamentalist Christian churches. You know the type, I'm sure. Them sorts of folks who's always in your face a-tellin' you what your business should be.

Them ones a-screamin' these days about how God created everything with his 'Intelligent Design'. I got a problem with this Intelligent Design shit. Explain how *it* explains a person like George Bush or that Yoko Ono for beginners. Not to mention that halitosis ol' Alligator spewed, or them fuckin' Portuguese man of wars a-stingin' my ball sack down the beach. Intelligent Design, my ass. Tell the truth, I think God seen what he created here on earth, then high-tailed it the fuck someplace else in the universe to try all over again to get it right. Anyways, at first I thought that with all the screechin' and a-hollerin' comin' from over yonder, that they's a-havin' ritual murders or some shit over that there wall. But no. Oh no. They was a-havin' people over and baptizin' them suckers in their Olympic-size swimming pool for chrissakes. Hallelujahs, I calls 'em. Now, all that dern commotion was bad enough, but when they starts a-showin' up at my door a-tryin' to fuckin' recruit me into their cult – a-goin' on 'bout how I'd better get my act together 'cause End Times is a-comin', and it's time to get ready for Armageddon – well, I got all ornery and pretty riled right quick. Now, I decides to have me a bit of a larkin' next time them Hallelujahs comes a-callin'. Surer than shit, those dead-eyed zombies invade my front door like the fuckin' Vietcong and come a knockin' once more – starts in a-tellin' me this and that 'bout the Bible and how it's the literal word of God. Bunch of 'em's got 'bout as much horse sense as a donkey. So, I says, literal word? That so, is it now? Well I been a-readin' that there Bible, ya see. Tarnation, I tells 'em, that good book's got more inconsistencies than the fuckin' IRS tax codes! Look through them pages, I tells 'em and explain how come God's a-givin' Jesus Christ two entirely different genealogies in Matthew and Luke, I says. Couldn't He at least get where his own son come from straight? And why does it say God created women from clay *and* from Adam's rib in Genesis? I mean, it must have been one or t'other. God sure as hell was there, weren't He? You'd think He'd get the details in His own book straight, a-seein' as He created the earth and the heavens above. Seein' as His design's so intelligent, now. Who knows, maybe God weren't too interested in a-writin' books. Maybe he moved on to screenplays. Now, them Hallelujah folks is a-standin' there a-lookin' cattywumpus on my front stoop when I says, y'know, thanks for droppin' by folks, but I ain't interested in a personal savior who can't take change from a cashier or do the breaststroke. Part of me wanted to give 'em all an ass-clockin' but I just smiled. Like I always says, if God invented everything, He sure as shit invented a sense of humor, so lighten the fuck up, people. Now, don't get me wrong. I'm as God-fearin' as the next fella. Back there over in Vietnam my motto was 'Praise the Lord and pass the ammunition!' Been a regular church-goer all my life. Barely ever missed a Sunday, but I'll tell you this, boy oh boy. All them churches a-springin' up 'round these parts lately, claiming they have the *one true way* to Christ, I mean, what the hell must poor old Jesus think about all the confusion He started? Then all this shit these Hallelujahs is a-preachin' about Jesus comin' back to take true believers to heaven and killin' everybody else who ain't a-cottonin' to His word. The Rapture, them Hallelujahs calls it. The time when ol' Jesus is a comin' back to kill whoever don't agree He's our Savior. Hearin' that shit makes me so dern ornery I'd like to throttle the fuckers. You don't never want to know what carnage and sufferin' I seen back there in the jungles of 'Nam. Ain't nothin' no how 'bout death to be worshippin' or glorifyin'. Then to be preachin' that our sweet Lord would turn into a killer. I told y'all I been reading them Biblical pages and from what I read, Jesus is love. Period. Ain't no murderin' intentions in that great man. I mean, come on. I ain't been no angel in my life, you know, but I believe Jesus will give me a big ol' hug when I stand before Him on Judgement Day – not a kick in the nuts. I mean, shit, life's fuckin' hard enough, ain't it? Who needs self-righteous motherfuckers here on earth who ain't never even been to heaven a-tellin' me what heaven's all about, for that matter? Shit, even with all that Doppler Radar shit the dang meteorologists can't predict what category fuckin' hurricane's a-comin'. Some Hallelujahs a-gonna tell me when Jesus is a-comin? Jesus will come back when He damn well wants to. So, as things often tend to do in life, events starts to escalatin' over there next door. All that Hallelujah a-hootin' and a-hollerin' goes from once a month to every fuckin' weekend. I was a-growin' more ornery than a goat's butt in a pepper patch 'bout it all. Now, my best buddy in these parts, that's Elias Esper. Old Esp has been my best friend since I moved back here-abouts after my hitch in the Marines was up back in sixty-nine. Well, old Esp is over a-visitin' me of a Sunday and says, 'Jesus jumping Christ, what in fuck-diddly's going on over that wall?' I brings him over to where there was a gap, and we takes a gander and seen them people a-jumpin' and a-screamin' and a-prayin' and a-duckin' under-water in that big ol' pool. Ol' Esp nudges me and says, 'For chrissakes, these fucking loudmouths are gonna give poor Jesus a headache. Don't they know that the switchboard to Christ connects through silent prayer?' Well, we gets to havin' another beer or two, and old Esp, now he's a smart one you know, college-educated up there in New England or Boston or some shit. The sun's a-goin' down in a blaze over the Gulf, and we hear that preacher a-rantin' from next door – screamin' on about some gloom and doom fire and brimstone from the Book of Revelation. Heared it so much it's seared into my memory: 'And I looked and behold, a pale horse . . .' Now, these fun-damentalists believe in the Apocalypse – Armageddon – the final destruction of the world as it's set down in them there Revelations. Only, old Esp tells me them ol' Revelations ain't got nothin' to do with the end of the world. Tells me that Revelation ain't a book of prophecy, that it's an attack in some sort of code, on the Romans who were givin' shit to the early Christians. That it's all about crap that went down like, two-thousand years ago, not shit's a-gonna happen in the future. It's all symbolic-like. He said that the only ones who could understand the code died about nineteen-hundred years ago, for chrissakes. Tells me them scribblers or whatever they called them – scribes – who put the Word of the Lord in book form fought long and hard about even includin' Revelation in the New Testament. Now, what ol' Esp told me next sort of shocked me. Esp tells me that the Old Testament, the Hebrew Bible, has not a word in it about heaven or an afterlife. Them ancient Jewish people in Israel didn't have that belief back in the day. They believed once you was dead, you was dead. Now, you never hear them preachers a-mentionin' that one, do ya'll? So I reads me the Bible again, and y'know, ol' Esp was right. I mean, God came first. What if Jesus was wrong about where he was ascendin'? Who came up with heaven as an idea if it weren't God? Maybe them UFO nut-jobs have a point when they talk about gettin' snatched or beamed up into outer space. 'Think of this too,' ol' Esp says, 'The Catholics are the ones who started the church in the first place, and the Catholics don't read the Bible,' he says. They have it interpreted for them by their priest. Now, it gets a little complicated, but from what Esp is a-tellin' me, when them Protestants began rebellin' against the Catholics five-hundred years ago, didn't nobody 'cept priests and maybe the Pope till that time take a gander through them biblical pages. I mean, shit, back then the Popes fucked anything that moved, so maybe they never bothered readin' it either. Fuck me dry, nobody could read till a few hundred years ago anyways 'cept the priests, ol' Esp tells me. Now, you put the Word of God into just anybody's ol' hands, and who knows what the fuck they'll come up with? You take a gander at what ol' George Bush has done with the glorious Constitution I fought so hard to protect way back when there in Southeast Asia. He's done with it what ol' Pinky done with her bananas, but I'll get to that in a minute. I mean, I remember when my second wife read page twenty-seven of *The Godfather* back in seventy-two, and virtually had a fuckin' orgasm a-readin' 'bout Sonny Corleone screwin' that bridesmaid. Though, from the looks of that ugly monkey face o' his, George Bush ain't never had an orgasm ever. Now, old Esp and me has always loved a good joke. Esp is one hell of a prankster, he is. He pulled a fast one on a shyster lawyer who screwed him over once. That was a pisser – involved a dead raccoon, ten gallons of Cool Whip and an industrial-sized dildo, but I'll tell you the details 'bout that some other time. So, I starts in a-complainin' to Esp about how I'm so fed up with a-callin' the cops about the screamin' and all t'other crazy goin's-on next door every fuckin' weekend. Me threatenin' them Hallelujahs with lawsuits and such, I mean, I'm about ready to go postal, and Esp gets an idea. I weren't too keen on it at first. Esp, I tells him, that dog won't hunt. Trust me, Esp says. That's how I comes to meet Pinky, you see. Pinky lives up over there in Wewahitchka nowadays at the circus performers' retirement home.

She's a-gettin' a bit up there in years – some of her teeth are falling out – but in her day she was the shinin' star of the circus. People came from far and wide to see that ugly ol' girl perform her amazing equestrian feats. Esp is a-telling me she was one of the best bareback riders he ever seen! Get that ol' girl on a horse, he says, and she'd make it leap over the fuckin' Empire State Buildin' for chrissakes. So, Esp comes over on a few consecutive weekends, and we starts a-cookin' up our little plan. Give them Hallelujahs next door one hell of a revelation, that's what we planned, sho 'nuff! Now, not long after that, we takes a drive up over to Wewahitchka to meet Pinky, and ask her manager if we can avail ourselves of her equestrian expertise for a weekend. I was a bit surprised when I first laid eyes on that ol' girl. I mean, I'd seen old photographs and stuff that Esp had shown me, and Pinky was always dressed to the nines in the most elegant costumes and sequined dresses. But, we goes into the circus performers' retirement village, and there she was, a-settin' in the sun bare-assed, them droopy old titties of hers almost a-draggin' in the sand while she's a-puffin' on a cigarette and stickin' a banana halfway up her ass. I about fainted dead away, boy, when she yanked that banana from her behind, shucked it, and chomped it down. Esp said she'd been a-doin' that sort of thing for years. Ever since she swallowed a billiard ball by mistake, that poor ol' girl had been makin' sure that whatever it was she was a-eatin' wouldn't have a rough ride out the other end, if you know what I'm a-sayin'? I mean, Pinky's a baboon after all. Can't expect monkeys to follow the same sorts of etiquettes as us humans now, can ya'll? So, some greenbacks pass hands with Pinky's manager, and off goes Pinky to stay with Esp on his ostrich ranch to get used to him for a week or two. Been a few years since ol' Pinky climbed up on a horse, so he gets her used to ridin' bareback again too – on a real beauty of a white filly. Teaches her some whistle commands and a little dance. I went up there one day to watch how things was a-progressin' and that fuckin' monkey was rejuvenated. I mean, she was a-smilin' from one tiny little ear to t'other. Ol' Pinky, she's about the tamest, sweetest varmint I ever did see. That monkey's as ugly as sin, but I wish any one of my wives had her disposition. We lets a few other ol' boys in on the plan, then on the Sunday we chose to strike, them Hallelujahs starts in a-screamin' and a-hollerin' as the sun goes down, right on cue, just like they been a-doin' for months and months. And always them same old lines from Chapter Six Revelations every fuckin' weekend, 'bout halfways through the sermon. Them ones about a pale horse and the beast. And there's Pinky in my garage, all done up a-lookin' like somethin' out of a horror movie – Esp studied that ol' Book of Revelations for accuracy, a-paintin' Pinky's face so she looked like the Devil himself. Stuck a fur stole on her so she'd look like the beast who was a lion, stuck horns on her head, strapped wings on her back, and that dang monkey never batted an eye. Just a-set there calm as could be, a-sippin' Diet Coke and a-chain-smokin' Marlboro Lights. Now, hereabouts, me and my buddies Jackass and Ponce de León climbs up on my roof. Now, see that big tree aside my house here a-cuttin' off the view from over next door? We could see them Hallelujahs, but they sure as shit couldn't see us. And then things gets to rockin' and rollin' next door. 'Oh Jesus!' They's a-chantin'. 'Hallelujah, Jesus!' and all this other caterwaulin'. Now, Ponce de León likes a nip or two and he was pretty smashed. Literally walkin' on a slant. Starts a-slippin' and a-slidin' on the asphalt shingles up there, and almost took a dive off the fuckin' roof just before the curtain's about to go up on our sideshow. Then that preacher starts in: 'And I heard a voice in the midst of the four beasts say . . .' Esp comes a-runnin' out from the garage with a big ol' grin and gives the signal. Surer than shit, he's a-holdin' the reigns of that fine white filly with Pinky on her back, I'm a-tellin' ya, almost give me a fright, seein' ol' Pinky up there a-lookin' like she's ready to guard the gates of hell itself. And the Preacher's a-swayin' over yonder beside the pool, a-preachin' to his brethren, a-yappin' and a-shoutin', 'And I looked, and behold a pale horse: and his name that sat on him was Death. And hell followed with him!' Old Esp gives me and the boys the hi-sign and we starts in, a-lightin' them fireworks like it's the fuckin' Fourth of July. There's bottle rockets a-flyin' through that tree there and explodin'. Ol' Jackass is a-hurlin' smoke bombs over yonder, and Ponce de León's a-tossin' M-8os by the handful into that fuckin'

Olympic-size pool. I mean, there hadn't been that many explosions 'round these parts since the War of Northern Aggression! Jackass is a-firin' them flare guns of his like he's John Wayne, and all them Hallelujahs is a-standin' there, eyes a-poppin', lookin' like they's about to shit their fuckin' shorts. I'm a-tellin' ya brother, it was gooder 'n grits! Then, Esp whups that horse's ass, and off she gallops with ol' Pinky a-standin' on her back and holdin' onto that filly's mane for dear life. Oh, what a sight! Ol' pro that she is, that fuckin' monkey worked that horse a few paces, then fixes to gettin' her into a gallop and off they fly – right over that there wall near that palmetto tree there. Now, I told you that ol' Esp told me Pinky could jump the Empire State Buildin' and he weren't kiddin', brother. Sho 'nuff, she overshot the wall a mite, and that fuckin' horse and her land right in the middle of that darned Olympic-sized pool, a-sendin' a splash so high you would have thunk a fuckin' asteroid had struck. Meanwhile, them fireworks is a-explodin' and them Hallelujahs is a-screamin and a-runnin' in every direction, yellin', 'Lord have mercy! The beast is among us!' We was all a-laughin' so hard, we's like to pee our pants. Now, I don't reckon baboons is too keen on a-gettin' wet, and ol' Pinky a-shoots out of that pool so fast, you'd have thunk that there water was on the boil. That filly's a-splashin' and a-neighin' and ol' Pinky's a-runnin' this way and a-that way, hootin' and a-monkey-gruntin'. Then that dang monkey whips off her pretty little devil dress there, and starts doin' a hoochie-coo 'round that preacher, shakin' them ol' droopy dugs o' hers like they's maracas, and a-doin' more pelvic thrusts than Madonna on Viagra! At that point the preacher faints dead away into the Olympic pool. Now, ol' Esp gives a few toots on a whistle, and Pinky scoots back over that wall lickety-split. We all high-tailed it into Roger's van with that crazy monkey, and drove out of there quicker than a rabbit fuck. From what I heard later, that poor filly shit a load so big in the pool it took two weeks to drain and clean the fucker. But that filly eventually climbed out of there with the assistance of the Apalachicola Fire department, and she was hunky-dory. Now, I'll tell you this, boy. It sure is a beautiful thing to have some genuine peace again in my golden years. Come back out here on this ol' patio of an evenin' and just enjoy the quiet these days. I'm a-tellin' y'all, I owe that monkey a heap of gratitude. Now, I have no idea how that little plan of Esp's worked on them Hallelujahs, but it sure did. Them dern Hallelujahs took their crazy-ass fundamentalism elsewheres, and I'm sure glad of that, boy. I don't even mind seein' that big ol' cross still a-standin' there over yonder. Sometimes I look at it and it reminds me of our Lord. Other times I pretend it's a clothesline post.

Fire Escape

JOHANNA FOSTER

My mother liked everything in the apartment to be neat and simple. Tables were cleared at the end of every day, throw blankets were tucked into drawers, toys were sorted into bins, which rolled away underneath my bed – our home was a row of compartments and doors into which things were filed, folded and stacked. Maybe, by hiding our belongings away, we felt we had more than we did.

The shape of our apartments was the same, but Anne Wright had a different relationship with space. Her things trickled out of every corner. Whenever she bought something new, everything had to be rearranged so that it could sit on display. As an item grew older, it shifted out of view until it ended up in boxes, shoved in corners, or, eventually, was thrown away.

We lived in a five-story building, between the rundown blocks of Hell's Kitchen and the sparkling open air of Lincoln Center. The building directly behind ours was a music school. During the first weeks of summer, before the heat was shut out to trap in air-conditioning, the sound of croaking violin strings and abrupt piano chords echoed in the wide alleyway between the buildings. The worst days were Fridays, when they held percussion classes. Hour after hour each class was allowed to bang, slam, pound, ring, and clash whatever instrument inspired them. At night, the building was dark and quiet, except when they held recitals at the end of each term. On those nights you could see into the lit rooms. I listened to awkward stage fright – skipped passages, blank time between musical phrases, speed playing, and the flushed performance of musical prodigy: nimble fingers and careful sustaining.

The alleyway that separated our buildings wasn't pretty or nice, but it was an oasis of walled-in concrete outdoor space. To reach it, I had to climb down our fire escape. Like in *West Side Story*, clamped to the side of every building on our block, was a repeating z, extending down into one of the eight alleyways. Each alley was shared by two buildings and separated from the others by brick walls, nearly ten feet high, and topped with barbed wire. I was one of few kids that had a safe place to play outside alone. Each spring my mother climbed down the fire escape steps with a hose and a bottle of bleach. First she cleared away the trash – she complained every year, watched like a hawk to see which window litter floated down from; there were always at least two bags full to carry to the curb. Then she covered each inch of cement and concrete with bleach before hosing it down. I knew that spring had begun from the antiseptic smell she brought back with her into the house. My outdoor toys – soap bubbles, a jump rope, balls, sidewalk chalk – were all stashed in a large plastic box on the fire escape. The fire escape also connected our apartment to the one directly above ours, where Anne lived.

My mother tried to stop me from just running up to see her every day. I sometimes waited for Anne to call, hoping she would invite me over, but I often forgot or grew impatient and just barreled up without permission. I didn't actually do much of anything during my visits. Anne didn't have any children, which made her different from all the other adults I knew. Sometimes we played games, but she was busy – doing laundry, cooking, cleaning, paying bills – and I was happy to sit and watch her, or to sit in the family room staring at her things. Sometimes she forgot I was in the house.

One night she found me sitting alone in the living room after sunset, too shy, too afraid of disturbing her home, to get up and turn on the light. She came in to close the windows, flicking on the lights, and jumped back, catching her breath, when she saw me sitting there.

'Rose! I had no idea you were there! Jesus! You scared me half to death. What are you doing sitting in the dark?'

I stared at the coffee table awkwardly, eyeing the candy bowl, the bits of paper, the little saucer holding change, and the stacks of opened mail with loose envelopes hanging raggedly off of them.

'My eyes adjusted. I can see everything.'

Anne tilted her head, smiling, puzzled. 'Why in the world didn't you just get up and turn on the light?'

I couldn't explain why, but just shrugged stupidly. She shrugged back laughing, 'You must have dozed off.'

I didn't answer but smiled dumbly. The next time it happened, I hid behind a chair when I heard her footsteps approaching

I loved the way her house smelled, like a home in constant motion: food – Pepsi – laundry – soap – steam – cigarettes – mint – plastic. It was warmer than our apartment, always a few degrees warmer, because it was one floor up and got more sunlight. The air was thicker with things, the people seemed larger, the furniture was bigger, and I could sit with my knees and ankles touching, small, unimportant and unnoticed, afraid to reach out and taint all that commotion.

While Anne didn't have children, she had dozens of nieces and nephews who came to visit. This was how my habit of visiting began. I was invited to play with the other children down in the alleyway behind the house. When they went upstairs to eat snacks and drink fruit punch, I joined them. While we were playing downstairs, it was understood that I could come and go as I pleased.

Anne took for granted that I slipped away from the games outside in order to avoid getting in trouble. What began with an hour of bouncing a handball against the wall would change when someone found an abandoned stick. Then stickball would adapt as someone discovered small rocks or chipped bricks from the wall. Finally, if no windows had been hit, and the neighbors hadn't yet begun to complain, they would try to lob balls, sticks, and rocks into open windows at the music school. I was always up the stairs and inside when they discovered the stick.

Adults have a tendency to confuse silence with manners or good behavior. My reluctance to talk, even to ask for a glass of water, made me seem obedient. And in truth, I would have done anything Anne asked of me in order to be able to spend time in her house. Maybe I liked her unbroken chatter, the way she spoke out loud – sarcastically or in parody of herself – as she rushed through the house. The other children kept me at a distance; they mistrusted my eagerness to spend time with grown-ups. For them, grown-ups were people who gave you things – toys, dolls, games, clothing, and people who stopped you from doing the things you wanted to do.

By the time I was eight, I was slipping out of my house nearly every day to go up to Anne's. In the summer, she left her windows open, and I could crawl in and out from the fire escape landing without anyone knowing that I was there. My mother assumed I was in my room playing, and Anne sometimes had no idea that I was there at all. Sometimes I only walked up the fire escape to her floor, without going in. I had to be careful climbing up. The beams would shake and echo if I didn't step lightly, and then my mother would hear, and crane her neck out the window.

The neighborhood looked different one flight up. I could see farther into the music school. From my apartment I could see only the upper half of walls, the outlines of ceiling molding. From Anne's floor, I could see into the rooms. The best part of any lesson was when the teacher played. An instrument that was being choked or spat into seemed softened and flawless in the teacher's hands. I could hear regret in whatever it was the child played next. Pianists handled their keys gently, violinists bowed lightly – they understood that they were doing their instruments a disservice. Once a girl threw a tantrum after her teacher played. Her shrieks were audible from the fire escape. 'If I had a grown-up violin, I could play like that too! It's because I have a baby violin! Give me your violin to play with!' She continued until the teacher took her instrument and played it, and it was even better. The little girl refused to bow for the rest of the lesson but played everything pizzicato, plucking her strings in frustration with her short fat fingers.

On the night of a recital, I went up the fire escape to see them playing. Families sat in straight rows facing the open area where the children were performing. Younger brothers and sisters sat on the floor at the front, squirming and poking each other. The recitals were always scheduled so that the best students went last, sometimes even in duets with their teachers, so I waited until the very end. By the time the recital was over, night had settled in. The lights across the street were dimming as the guests left, and finally even the recital area went black. I made my way downstairs as quickly as possible.

I could see the light from my kitchen below when the step gave out underneath my foot. All my weight was on that foot, and in the darkness, in the confusion of a slowed down moment, all I registered was the sudden absence of resistance beneath my feet and the stinging pain of a metal bar in my palm. I howled for my mother. When she came outside she found me dangling above her. Anne ran to her window, switching on the light, and illuminating the fire escape. I could see now where the step had been. I had flung myself five feet forward and up. As my mother, shaking and crying, helped me down, she asked me over and over again, 'How in the world did you get up there?' Thankful to have my hand back, happy to be out of danger, I kept reassuring her, 'I don't know, Mom. Really I swear.'

After my mother inspected every inch of me for cuts or bruises, injuries she couldn't believe I had escaped, she shook her head in disbelief. 'God, you were lucky. I don't want you out on the fire escape again.'

'But I'm fine, Mom. Nothing happened.'

She was still shaking her head. 'I don't want you using the fire escape. Promise me you won't go out on there anymore.'

'But I'm fine. I caught myself.'

'I still don't know how you managed that. God, I think your guardian angel must have been watching over you tonight. Just promise me you won't go out there again.'

I rolled my eyes, pouting, and she raised her eyebrows expectantly. 'You're going to have to stay in the house from now on. And that's final.'

In our bathroom, I could hear conversations from other apartments. I pictured the pipes snaking behind our walls like hollow telephone lines. I lay on my back in the bathtub, face up to the spout, holding it with my hand to pull my face out of the water. The spout was dark and nubby green on the inside. I began in whispers. Maybe if I reminded Anne that I was downstairs, she would call and invite me up. I whispered her name, 'Anne', cupping my hands around my mouth, so that my mother wouldn't overhear. I waited for long seconds between each try, but no replies came. Maybe she wasn't hearing my whispers. Maybe it wasn't loud enough.

'Hello! Hello!' I shouted. 'Hello! Can you hear me?'

My mother knocked gently on the door, 'Honey, is there something you need?'

'Umm. I can't find my yellow face towel.'

'It's in the red box on the shelf!'

'Thanks.'

'Don't stay in there much longer, honey. You'll get all pruney.'

I imagined Anne walking around her apartment, oblivious to the shouts coming up her bathroom faucet.

What I missed most about my visits upstairs was the return home afterwards, the slow descent from the cluttered warmth of Anne's apartment, to the cool familiar silence at home. Tucked in bed that night, I could hear my mother and Anne, sitting on the fire escape and gossiping. They sat together for hours, whispering and laughing. Anne's laugh was louder and more distinct than my mother's. My mother has a tendency to swallow her laughs, as if she is out of breath, but Anne cracked her jaw open and let it belt out. The alleyways behind our building brought the conversation round in pockets.

I could make out bits and pieces of it. My mother's voice, '– and then they're planning on tearing down the cinema… building huge condos or something…' and Anne's voice, 'I say let them. Maybe our landlord will finally have to fix up this place; but remember when they said they were going to tear down the projects and build?' and again her laughter booming through the window. I fell asleep with it ringing in my ears.

Weeks passed, and I waited for Anne to call, but she didn't. I tried once to call Anne while Mom wasn't looking. I knew her number by heart. I had been made to memorize it in case of emergencies. I let it ring five times, but no one picked up. I would get in trouble if Mom found out I had called and let it ring more than five times. 'Sometimes people don't pick the phone up because they don't want to be bothered,' she would say. I placed the receiver back on its cradle. My mother found me later, putting a puzzle together on my floor.

'Almost bedtime, Rose. You better start putting your toys away.'

'Mommy, can I learn to play the piano?'

She looked at me in surprise, 'The piano? Honey, we can't afford a piano. And where in the world would we put it?'

'We wouldn't need to buy one. I could practice on a keyboard. Or maybe they would let me practice at the music school when no one's there. Like in the morning before school.'

'If you want to play the piano, you need to have a piano. We haven't got the money for lessons anyway. Aren't you learning the recorder in school right now? I never hear you practice that. A piano is a big expensive commitment.'

'But the recorder is awful. It's so squeaky and terrible.'

'All instruments sound squeaky in the beginning. Why don't you try practicing more and see if it doesn't start to sound nicer. Anyway, it's time for bed. Clean up your toys and get ready.'

My mother took off work early my last day of school before Christmas break. We had a half-day and parents were invited to come and see the classroom. She ran late, though, and arrived only in time to walk me home. It was cold outside and by the time we got there, I couldn't feel my hands. As I locked the door behind us – turning three bolts in a row along the edge of the frame and shifting the huge metal pole into its cradle in the floor – I felt the frozen skin peeling away from my fingertips.

After taking off my outside layers, I pulled a book from the shelf and settled on the living room couch. And then I heard the noises upstairs. Loud pounding through the floor – grinding, slamming, and four pairs of feet. I counted them. I could tell which were Anne's feet, but didn't know whom the others belonged to. My mother was pulling open the curtains.

'Mom, what's going on upstairs?'

She didn't turn to me, but continued carefully tying the curtains back.

'What do you mean, honey?'

'Can I go upstairs, Mom?'

'I'm sure Anne is busy right now, honey.'

'Busy doing what?'

'Rose, you can't just go upstairs when Anne is busy.'

I waited for the noise to quiet down, but at three, it hadn't. And then I finally understood that something extraordinary was taking place upstairs. My mother was folding laundry in the kitchen.

'Mom, what is all that noise upstairs?'

'Rose, I told you not to bother Anne today.'

My mother only ever kept information from me 'for my own good', and I hated it. There never seemed to be any relief in not knowing something. Most of the time I managed to find out on my own. Sometimes I listened in on her phone calls, or asked clever questions that made her slip, but this time I was stuck. The only way to find out what they were hiding from me was to go upstairs, which I wasn't allowed to do.

I couldn't think of any other way to be heard above the scraping and thumping upstairs, so I let go. I kicked and screamed and howled. I threw things, things I really cared for, sent Benjamin the Bear flying, smashed my porcelain tea set against the wall, ripped at the hair of my doll, threw my very favorite books out into the hallway. My mother walked away from me, and I kicked the walls and doors, stubbed my toes, and listened to the ringing in my ears. She finally responded, wrapping me up in arms I couldn't break free of. I shrieked in her ears until she finally said it.

'She's moving.'

All of Anne's things fit into two small vans. It seemed impossible. I stood with my mother on the sidewalk, red eyes, arms and feet covered in raw tender bruises from hammering at the walls, holding onto my mother's legs. Before climbing into the van, Anne came over to us.

'Goodbye, I'll miss having you one floor down.'

I reached out, tugging at her arm. She looked at me now, smiling.

'And what will I do without you, Rose? You know, I'm moving into a big new house. It's so big that I'll have a big guest room. And guess who that's for?'

I stared at the sidewalk.

'It's so that you can come to visit. I can come pick you up anytime you want. The first thing I'm going to do when I move in is paint the room yellow, your favorite color. What do you think of that?'

'Can I come now?'

She would have said yes. I think she might have, but my mother pulled me a bit closer to herself, 'Rose, you have to wait till Anne is all moved in.'

Anne leaned in and gave me a hug. She put her arms around my waist, but I was holding on so tightly to my mother's leg that she ended up hugging my mom's knee too. As she pulled away, I whispered in her ear, 'Did I bother you too much?'

Before she could answer, her brother was yelling from the van, 'Come on now, we gotta go.' She kissed me on my forehead and ran up to the van, climbing in without looking back.

My mother and I headed inside. My toys lay in ruins in the hallway. The walls were scuffed from my shoes. My tea set was in shards near the door. My mother lifted me over them to tuck me into bed.

'It's okay if we clean those up tomorrow. Sleep tight, Rose.'

She walked carefully across the room, turning off the light before closing the door. I lay in bed, and could feel tingling heat in my feet. I heard her doing the dishes in the kitchen. She stacked them into the cabinet as she dried them. And then I heard her opening the back door and stepping out onto the fire escape.

Checkout

ANNA MURPHY

Tricia arrives at work early. The supermarket is at the edge of town, just a ten-minute walk from her parents' house, but she is anxious to get away. On Christmas Eve, even the supermarket is quieter than the house, with the others home from school, fighting over the television and getting Con excited. Tricia lights a cigarette and leans against the gable end of the supermarket warehouse, one leg making a triangle with the wall. She soaks up the few minutes of solitude, exhaling deeply and letting the smoke mix with a sigh, watching them both hang softly in the cold.

In front of her is the supermarket car park, and beyond that the bus stop and the main road to Dublin, the road that splits the whole town in two. This is some town, Tricia thinks, as the Dublin bus goes by. Just one bus going out, then the same one coming in. Still, at least it will bring Frankie and the others back this evening; at least that'll be something.

Tricia looks across the road, beyond the playing fields, to her old secondary school. It looks old and wise, the remnants of a mist still hanging low around it, the windows staring out. She counts to the window third from the left on the ground floor, the window Mr Kavanagh used to peer through during career guidance.

'Ladies,' he used to say, his hands cupped behind his back, his body leaning into the window, 'It'll be the bus or the supermarket.' Then he nodded wisely, 'Depending on what ye do now with these few years. Either the bus or the supermarket.'

He congratulated Tricia with a formal handshake and some words of wisdom when she scraped into college and earned her place on the bus. But now when he sees her at the checkout he doesn't say much. He just buys streaky bacon and stewing steak and floury spuds and cans of Guinness and disposable razors. When he hands over the money, he never says anything at all.

Tricia looks at her watch. Five minutes before her shift starts. If she were still in Dublin, she'd just be getting out of bed now, thinking about packing for the bus this afternoon. It felt great, Tricia remembers, swanning into town for a visit, knowing she'd be swanning out again as soon. The place didn't seem so bad then, when the bus pulled in, the Christmas lights dousing the streets in colour and the condensation blurring out the edges of the town, making it all just a soft sort of mush, the supermarket car park a mess of hats and scarves and headlights. She remembers the weight of her rucksack as she swung it onto her back, and the cold walk home to her family's terraced house in the middle of the town, stopping in on her daddy having his Christmas Eve drinks in Flanagans. That was the best part of those two Christmases, Tricia thinks, seeing her daddy in Flanagans. He looked like he could burst when he saw her coming into the bar, grabbing the other lads on the arms and rattling them to attention.

'Oh, look on, lads!' he beamed. 'The scholar returns!'

And they all looked up for a minute.

'She's back now to give us some educating over the Christmas dinner.'

He had squeezed her up all tight, smelling of sweat and porter, then he held her back at arm's length, had a good look at her, and started laughing. It always seemed a joke to him that she was going to college, some little miracle that he couldn't fathom, so he shook his head and laughed at it instead.

Tricia crushes out her cigarette and wonders about this evening, whether or not she should stop in to Flanagans. But she knows she won't, not on her way home from the supermarket. It wouldn't be the same at all.

Tricia sits at the till looking down the long queue, every trolley piled high. It will be a long day, but will help pay for the presents she had to buy: a toy truck and toolbox for Con, and jewellery for her mother and sister, for helping out with the babysitting. She just got small things for the others, only joke things really, but she hopes they won't mind; they know how it is. Nothing like when she stacked shelves as a kid; that wage was just a luxury, all spent on clothes and make-up. Frankie and Jen had been jealous of her then. They weren't allowed to work at all and Frankie was outraged, putting on a snooty face and propping her hand on her hip, imitating her mother.

'Frankie!' Frankie had mimicked. 'You have to concentrate on your studies! And you have all the clothes a girl could possibly need.'

Tricia had recounted the whole funny episode to her mother after school. But it sent her mother into a rage and the dinner preparations were punctuated by clattering pots and exclamations.

'Some people think their kids are too good for getting jobs!' her mother said. 'It's fine for those girls anyway – won't they all swan away to college. How did you ever end up making friends with that lot anyway?'

The girl to Tricia's left takes her break and taps Tricia on the arm, asking if she wants anything.

'A new job?' Tricia suggests.

'I'll be out of this kip soon enough alright,' the girl says. 'Just ten more months in this town and then I'll be in college.' Tricia tries to keep her smile stretched tight as the girl slopes off.

'I hope it works out for you,' Tricia mutters. She knows the minute she says it that Liz McGrath, the girl to her right, has heard.

Liz is the town's mothership of information and every scrap of gossip is funnelled through the narrow aisle by Liz's till.

'That one's got notions she has,' Liz says, her hands busy bleeping everything through and her satisfied eyes settling on Tricia.

'Nothing wrong with notions, is there?' Tricia asks.

Liz is scarcely a year older than Tricia and went straight to the supermarket after school. Tricia sees her sometimes whispering to shoppers, nodding over towards her, using her to prove some point about notions. Liz calls to the girl as she comes back from her break.

'Dearbhla,' she says. 'Didn't you know that Tricia sitting there beside you went to college herself? She could probably give you some advice about it all.'

Dearbhla looks horrified that someone who has gone to college is sitting at a checkout, and Tricia sighs at the thought of explanation. She thinks of telling her about it all, about having to work full-time to pay her way, about struggling with the exams, about repeating the year, about meeting a guy who seemed nice, just one guy. But she knows the details don't matter to anyone.

'I just fucked the whole thing up. I got pregnant and I fucked the whole thing up.' Dearbhla stares at her with her mouth open.

'I'll be going back though,' Tricia says. 'When Con, my baby, is older and I've saved some money.' She gives a little wave of her hand. 'All this,' she says, 'is just a temporary measure.'

Tricia plays games to pass the time, watching the shopping coming down, not looking at the customer, and trying to figure out what kind of person owns the shopping. She looks at some shopping coming down now and figures it's someone doing a last-minute Christmas dash, a woman with a job no doubt, and a car, buying luxury chocolates and lovely wine, and she bleeps it through. And there's Frankie standing in front of her with her hand on her hip saying, 'OhmygodTricia! Tricia! What the hell are you doing here?'

It takes Tricia a minute to register that it's Frankie. She's draped in some sort of cashmere shawl and her hair is straightened and shiny and she looks so elegant that Tricia can hardly place her for a second.

'What are you doing here?' Frankie asks again.

'Working, of course.' Tricia rolls her eyes and forces a laugh. 'Con started playschool a few months ago, so I can work in the mornings now, and Julie's helping me out for Christmas, and mam minds him for a few hours when she can. So here I am!'

'Oh. Wow.'

'God Frankie, I would never have recognised you from your shopping.'

Frankie looks confused and shrugs.

'Weren't you always one for six packs of cider and bumper packets of HobNobs?' Tricia continues. 'What are you doing with decent wine and posh chocolates?'

'Ah Tricia,' Frankie says. 'Them good ol' student days. Sure aren't they long gone!'

'You shouldn't be here at all yet,' Tricia says, trying to explain away her surprise, 'The bus doesn't get in for ages.'

'I drove down, silly. I got a car. Remember?' But Tricia doesn't remember – doesn't think Frankie even told her – and then Frankie is packing up and moving away.

'Better not hold up the queue! See you tonight?'

'Yeah, I think I can get out. Where?'

Frankie scrunches up her face. 'Didn't you get the email? Oh, of course not! McCarthys. Around eight. See you then.'

The queues get even longer after Frankie's gone, and the noise gets even louder. Everyone's wishing everyone Happy Christmas, and the same Christmas songs are playing over and over, and the bleeps from all the scanners seem constant, like it's all just one big long bleep, as if the whole place is flatlining and soon all the tills will just pack up and die. And underneath it all, in some forgotten part of her head, Tricia hears Frankie's voice, the way it was in college, telling her it would all work out okay, that she'd get back to college sometime, that they'd share a flat again, that they'd all help out with the baby.

'Tricia,' Liz says, 'did your friend not even know you had a job?'

'No. She's not home all that often.'

'Isn't that what phones are for?'

'Yeah, but mobiles are expensive and I can't be affording to ring people every time anything happens.'

Tricia wonders whether Frankie uses her phone much and if she worries about the bills.

'That was nice stuff she was buying,' Liz interrupts again. 'Not her usual shopping, though.'

'What do you mean?'

'She normally buys stuff for the week. Those ready meals, y'know, microwave dinners for one. Sometimes a bit of salad as well, and some sausages and rashers and that. And she has a sweet tooth: loads of biscuits and crisps and cakes. And she buys those SlimFast shakes as well. She was a bit podgy in school, wasn't she? And she always buys wine too. Plenty of wine!'

'How would you know what Frankie buys?'

'Sundays,' Liz says. 'On her way to Dublin. Shops closed I guess by the time she gets back up there. She's been in a good few Sundays since she got the car.'

Tricia doesn't say anything to Liz then. She's doing the mental maths, trying to figure out how often Frankie rang to say she was home, and how often Tricia couldn't meet her because of the baby. How often did she drop in for a visit? There had to have been times so when she didn't ring or call at all.

But there's more shopping and more bleeping and the talk and the music close in on Tricia's head, until she can hardly think at all, until all there is is noise, and the whole place is flatlining and she feels like she's in a trance. Is this what it's like?, she wonders. After years of just bleeping and nodding and bagging, is it all just like a trance?

The pub is busy by the time Tricia gets there and she makes for the corner where her crowd, the college crowd, would normally be. Liz spots her moving through and gives her a wave, watching Tricia as she finds her group. Frankie's sitting in between Jen and Michelle, with a few others who Tricia doesn't know so well huddled around. Tricia squeezes onto the edge of a bench beside Jen, who makes a bit of a fuss of her at first, counting back to think when she saw her last and saying how it must be six months and isn't that awful and they're all just so busy with jobs and boyfriends and houses and everything else. Jen gets pulled into other conversations, about the deposit Michelle has down on an apartment, and Ann-Marie's boyfriend wanting her to move in with him, and Frankie's bonus structure in her new job. Almost an hour goes by and Tricia says nothing, just nods along to the stories, trying to piece together the pictures of their lives, like she's learning about some other breed of humans. She listens and drinks.

As the rush of news dies down they turn to Tricia, asking her questions. She shrugs and opens and closes her mouth, as if she's doing an interview but hasn't prepared any of the answers. She tells them about how Con is getting on at playschool, but Frankie's eyes glaze over and Jen just smiles sort of goofy and Michelle goes to the bar. So she tells them about the job, and they nod and cluck and look sad.

'But it's funny too,' Tricia says, disconcerted by the sympathetic looks. 'You can tell all sorts of things by watching what people buy. Everything really: age, sex, weight, who's single, who's married – whatever.'

For the first time all evening, Tricia has everyone's attention. So instead of telling them about Con and her everyday life, she tells them about the shopping.

'This guy came in a few weeks ago, buying the usual groceries; he's not living at home with his mam or anything. But as well as the tea and the bread and that he has a load of all this preening stuff, razors and smellies and nail clippers and hair wax. Liz says he never buys all that stuff so we reckon he's getting ready for some hot date. So we keep an eye out to see what he's getting the next few times, how he's getting on with yer woman and all. So there he is a few days later...

putting in a bunch of flowers with the usual things. Another day then a box of chocolates. He's in again then last week and all of a sudden there he is buying all this stuff he has never bought before, air freshener and supersoft toilet paper and candles, getting ready to have her over y'know, wine in the basket instead of beer. And what else is in there with his shopping only a fuck-off bumper pack of johnnys. Arrogant shit, thinks we're anyone's for a bit of fancy toilet paper and he swaggers off then with his bags bursting out as wide as his trousers.'

She looks around the circle, gathering up the cackles, and head-throws and eye-rolls, and they're saying 'dirty bugger', and 'all the same' and 'isn't he right?'

Frankie says, 'I'm his for the wine and the chocolate', so there's more laughing then and everyone's teasing Frankie about her latest fling with some guy in the office. Tricia looks at Frankie laughing, and thinks of all the boyfriends Frankie's had, all the guys she's been with, and she wonders why it wasn't Frankie, or one of the others who fucked it up.

'Jesus, I'll never do my shopping in this town,' Jen says, letting on all shocked and proper. 'Who knows what you'd say about me, Tricia!'

Michelle laughs and wants to know more about the categories and the types and Tricia looks at them all laughing.

'There are all sorts,' Tricia says. 'Even a few yuppies.'

'What?' Jen says. 'There's no such thing as yuppies any more! And they wouldn't be in this town.'

'Yes, they are. They're building huge houses out in the country. They spend a fortune. All those gourmet ingredients – rocket leaves and sundried tomatoes and toasty ciabatta, stuffed pasta and pancetta and feta cheese. No such thing as sliced pan and easy singles. They buy all the expensive toiletries as well, the super soft toilet paper, and the pink razors for her, and the black razors for him. And wine, lots of wine. Nice wine, too.'

'Tricia!' Jen says. 'That's all the stuff I buy!'

'Really?' Tricia says, not surprised in a way. 'Ah y'see!' Tricia says, trying to smile. 'Not even two years out of college and you're a yuppie already.'

'What's wrong with all that stuff?' Jen says. 'It's just normal stuff.'

'Normal?' Tricia says. 'I wouldn't call it normal.'

'It's just different,' Frankie says.

'What do you mean different?' Tricia asks.

'Just different people buy different stuff,' Frankie replies. 'Different people like different stuff.'

Tricia thinks about the things she buys; the own brand baby food, the bumper packs of wipes, the 2-for-1 biscuits. Tricia doesn't like any of that stuff, that's not what she wants to buy at all. And this week she wanted to buy Con a big sit-in truck instead of the small one that she got, and she wanted to buy presents for all the family, and she wanted to buy wine and chocolates. But she can't buy all that, all that different stuff she likes.

'That's right,' Tricia says. 'Different people buy different stuff. And ye're just lucky that ye can afford to buy certain different stuff instead of certain other different stuff. Ye're just lucky that's how it went and that ye're buying the leaves and the tomatoes and not the nappies and the biscuits.'

It all comes out in a blur and Tricia laughs and drinks some more. She sees Frankie watching her, with her face all scrunched up and snooty, and Tricia thinks of Frankie in her apartment with her job and her clothes and all the shopping that Liz says she buys and Tricia's head is bleeping and throbbing and heavy. She hears someone changing the subject, but Tricia hasn't finished.

'But I haven't told you about all the categories! I have to tell you about one last type of shopper – the worst shopper of all – the desperado.'

They all go quiet then, looking at her like they don't want to hear any more about the shoppers after all.

'The desperados, the lonely singletons, who live all on their own. They have no one at all, which makes them buy food, lots of comforting food. Chocolate, and crisps and biscuits. Then they bung in a load of SlimFast or shit like that to try and make up for all the crap, in case they get fat. They buy microwave dinners, just for one, for every day of the week, because they've no one to feed but themselves.

And they buy some salad stuff too, to make up for buying the ready meals, and the crap, and the SlimFast.'

Tricia half-looks at Frankie then, just flickers her a look, but Frankie is staring out into the middle of the pub, her eyes shielded by her hair, her legs crossed and a slinky sandal bobbing off a pedicured toe.

'Shampoo for lanky greasy hair. Paracetamol for hangovers. Fags for the nerves. Sausages and rashers for another lonely Sunday morning. And biscuits… just in case anyone ever does call over, or some fella stays the night. And wine, lots and lots of wine. But good wine.'

Tricia sips her drink and listens to the silence, that different sort of silence, the silence that there is when everything has changed.

'I'm sick of this place,' Frankie says to the others. 'I'm sick of this grotty little pub. I don't know why we always come here. Let's go on to Mulligans or somewhere else.' Frankie gathers up her bag and coat and leads the procession to the door, ignoring Tricia all the time.

'Are you coming, Tricia?' Michelle asks, the last in the line of leavers, looking back as she goes.

'Nah,' Tricia says finishing off her drink. 'I'm going to talk to a few of the others,' she says, pointing over towards Liz and the supermarket crowd.

'I might follow ye on,' Tricia says to herself as the door swings shut.

Poems from
Man Imitating a Cloud

ERIK VATNE

Everything is OOOO

for Lou Reed

i like wrongness
it's recalcitrant
composition is like that
i don't particularly like dogs
horrible sort of *squish squish squish*
sometimes you'll see someone with nothing on
but a Band-Aid
there's just some sense of straining
you want to go someplace else
you really have to face that thing
and that's what all this is a little bit about
there's a point between what you want people to know about you
and what you can't help people knowing about you
there are always two things that happen
everything is Oooo
a whore i once knew
was a little bit like being Jean Shrimpton
i mean you had this feeling
in the summer he sold Good Humors
i suppose a lot of these observations
carry some slight magic
i'm sure there are limits
you pass through boredom
into fascination
it fixes them in a way

Party Baby!

al nyc nj ak fl ar Ca cO ct dC ga Ks hi id il in az ia ky la me md ma mi mn ms mo mt ne nv nh nm ny nc nd oh ok or pa ri sc Sd dE tn tX us vt va wa wv wi wy Brooklyn queens houSton phoenix antonio diego Philadelphia chicago Female Single available looking dating I like guys & bisexual females nude naked tanning kinky offline to party roleplay webcam net meeting cam photos pictures pic college parties phone beer keg sensual sexy massage online fun vibrator toy foot fetish videos meet Xtc fantasy bar lust 420 bud powered pix pics avis jpegs gifs video clips blonde horny tantra voyeur exhibitionist pose 69 camera film movies College Student exotic dancer erotic model operator agent escort flight attendant stripper dom video phone sex actress amateur Army navy air force marines coast guard reserves cops police officers firemen luv guys in uniform free tease wet panties ebony black sex cam men xxx dorm frat mp3 See soon in hustler penthouse playboy icu icuii mpeg thongs bikini lace bra

A Valediction Forbidding Mourning

i.m. Joe Strummer

Whatever happened to the Sandinistas?
It was such a beautiful word. I think of the actor
Ben Affleck's character in that crap film called *Bounce*
With Gwyneth Paltrow when he mocks out
Whitman's *When Lilacs Last in the Dooryard*
Bloomed. What the fuck is a dooryard anyway
He wants to know. I'd never thought of it like that
Before. I'm a polite well-mannered anarchist
Obsessed with rules of etiquette. I even play
A well-tempered clavier when the mood indigo
Strikes. The green tea is hot and has a thick oily
Taste. In my dream I heard Joey Ramone shouting
Gabba Gabba Hey Ho with the wind and the rain.
Rat poison courtesy of Chatterton. I'll have the tekka
Makki roll. Too bad it's not shoals of fishes again tonight.
The wedding guests want butternut squash soup.
What is a shoal father? Don't you stop and think
About what you're saying? If I had a nickel for every
Soda-jerk that tried to sell Joseph Cornell a ticket
To the peep show I'd be a rich man. An explosive
Spittoon is the last thing you'll ever hear from me.

Monk Playing a Cello

'He feeleth the same passions that my lackey doth...'
                                                    Montaigne

Beaten down by embolisms
A bonfire don't put it out of the house
Chalk it up to the outline of what the sidewalk never was
A form of unfamiliar faces squinting in the sunlight
Faces pressed up against glass
Breathe on it make a mark usually initials
Some sort of sign that fades with the heft of fear
Day's donkey-like in labial pharmacology labs
Kit Smart snugs in the bovine monodrama
Rattle of what remains of your leather interior
Ta is not the tee-tee of this musical manifesto
Unless of course you cancel the solvent cellos
Watch them unwind in a wind of salt and kayak
This thing that won't let me alone for a fig

Dun Scotus on His Sickbed

Green and yellow wind
breaker on bicycle
in Reykjavik. Segovia
lugging jugs of kerosene
to the skiff. Science
is so creepy sometimes.
A concertina
of gold and metallic
aqueducts ding
the conductor's windshield.

Keep as New

For my son, Dylan

Keep as new
the lapis lazuli snuff bottle
brought back from China
on the shelf
of the unpainted naked bookcase
I painted one day while drunk
when I lived in Rhinebeck
and had a wife and son
and we listened to gamelan music
in the summer and heard
the loud calling of the frogs
in the marsh

my wife started a collection
of frogs all kinds some from Bali
or Tasmania I tried hard to write a poem
about the frogs I tried hard
to be a man and love
it was like the real life
the one I squandered back there in the dense tussock
where I threw the wedding ring and waited
for the sky to lighten
so I could crawl on my hands and knees
searching like that
as if in prayer

from Devotions

I got something out of it you got something out of it let's not kid
    each other
I was okay while it lasted it was the cat's meow I made this for you
    with soot and spit
I sandblasted my emergency funds out of the keepsake sepulchre
Why is it always something anything why does it all come back to that
After all these years when I want it to be about Everything when I
    want it to be Yes
Let's check it out and see if it's still on my radar this thing that separates us
It isn't me or you or us or even Her it is Other it is the secret room I
    inherited
From my father the one you found out about even though the key was
    swinging
Back and forth on the chain of my heart you were Medea enough to
    suss it out
And intuit it into your own heart gullet entrails intestines and blood
    brain barrier
My smoke and mirror lust was not laughter and you weren't my
    daughter anymore
To love is to die in this life and Las Vegas ourselves into the Antediluvian
    orchestra
I can testify to untold and indeterminate lassitudes late night phone
    calls to pharmacies
It's all part of Plan A and Plan B it's all part of the needle piercing the
    skin of actual fact

75

And me of course making a sand *mandala* out of my imaginary lover
and sweeping it into the wind

What else possesses me to sacrifice the trance that doesn't last as long
as it used to

And yet and yet and yet and yet and yet and yes I stutter and stammer
out the guttural cries

The lariat whip and sing of each Gloria in the backseat of a Buick Skylark
Excelsis Deo

It's true I am Akhenaton and all the constellations are jism jettisoned
chiaroscuro across

The Satyr's lap and all my wives lovers' mothers and children satellites
of love orbiting around me

Oh I cannot name the stars my father taught me when I was a child
in Schraalenburgh

I can only remember when summer meant summer and my mother's
katydids made humid music in the trees

And the pungent smell of pot smoke wafted up like incense from a
priest-shaken censer

And honeysuckle creosote fresh cut grass like my first come blue light
from the bug zapper buzzing loud in the moonlight

Hosannas of *la petite mort* in my dreams I speak French even though
I don't baby baby baby

I get lost and weave these tender devotions out of what it is I set out
to say to you arabesque-wise

The rain has taught me all of that everything I referred to earlier and
down it falls

I open my window and wet my face with it and when I wipe it with
your torn thin tunic

I am open to all that this love allows as it lances each suture of our
wounded animals

Until finally when the fast balm is anointed and the light squibs at
the next world

What we thought we heard said back there in this entire hullabaloo
will be misread

And the first nothing and not this thing it is or was or ever will be
if you ever get to it

As arpeggios of rain falling on the rooftop *diminuendo* into visions
of forgotten grief

The sacrificial goat bleats and at last the sunlight breaks through the
clouds

And Capricorn makes a Marriage out of the five primrose
Hermaphrodites on Fire

Last Breath

i.m. of my father

All the books in that case
won't save me from my sad life.

A fracture takes place.

Last night, perfection.
I unrolled the papyrus
and translated my way
back into your last breath.

His Lordship Takes Aim

JONATHAN COOPER

It was only after I had shot my butler that it occurred to me there was no one to serve the second course. This was, at best, remiss of me, for I had an insatiable hunger that soup and bread had failed to satisfy. Leaning my chair back onto two legs, I stretched out my foot and gave the valet's thigh a kick, though I bore in mind not to kick too heartily, as my gout had been playing up and I'm awfully sensitive to pain. My nudging provoked no response, and so I set my chair upright and ruminated on my unenviable position. After some minutes, I judged starvation a more fitting end than having to suffer the indignity of serving my own dinner. I have been served throughout my life and was not about to start serving now. Even the fact that I could smell meat roasting through the stench of cordite would not sway me to move from my seat.

This abysmal predicament would, of course, never have come about if I hadn't bought my pistol in the first place. But I do not rue my decision, by God, and I never will. I have always believed regret to be a sign of weakness. If a man cannot stand by his decisions in life, then he doesn't deserve the privilege of making them. Take my luncheon, for instance. I had insisted on pork, although I had always preferred fish on a Tuesday, and if it's pork I chose then it's pork I shall have, and dash the consequences. The same goes for the purchase of my gun. Yes, if I had not bought it, I would still have my job and Betsy wouldn't have left me and taken the children to live in the Cotswolds. Yes, the butler would still be alive and I would be enjoying my tender and succulent roast. But that still does not mean I was wrong in buying my gun.

I rang the bell for some minutes to summon the cook, believing she may have had some rudimentary training in the arts of the silver service, or perhaps had been instructed by the valet in such matters, should he ever have fallen ill. Then I remembered that I had had to let her go due to penury.

A thought occurred to me. If I did not have a cook below stairs, who the devil was preparing my lunch? I sat and pondered this for some minutes, but was unable to reach a satisfactory conclusion. I once more attempted to rouse the butler, thinking perhaps he could have enlightened me, but the bowl of fruit that stood on the table was soon empty of apples, and henceforth I had nothing left to throw at him save my soup dish. I could never stand fruit. Too acidic for my constitution. And as the bowl was a Clarice Cliff I was reluctant to use it, fearing I might miss my supine retainer and shatter it on the floor, which was a bally disgrace anyway, seeing the maid had gone the same way as the cook.

Oh, how I missed Betsy. She was so much better at managing the domestics. I would always prefer to relax in the parlour, snug in my favourite armchair with pipe in mouth and paper in hand, than to dictate chores to the housemaid, who was a dull-witted woman and often tried my patience. Why bother chatting to a half-wit, I would say to Betsy over breakfast, when the finest minds of the age air their opinions in *The Times*? She merely tutted and returned to her kedgeree.

I missed the children too. Oh, how they used to scream and run about the garden when I took drunken pot-shots at them from the parlour window. As I looked around the dining room, it seemed that everything my eye fell upon brought to me some memory of their innocent, carefree ways. Emily's teddy sitting dusty and unhugged on the sideboard, or the bloodstained chip in the corner of the table where little Ralph had tripped and given himself the scar. I remember their faces when Betsy had taken them away, even though they were difficult to discern through the windows in the lounge, which had not been cleaned for several weeks. The children seemed as if they did not care. How Betsy used to urge me to play games with them or read them to sleep, for soon they would be grown and such simple pleasures would be lost forever. The indifferent look upon their small faces made me think that perhaps I had been wrong, that there was indeed something I had missed. How sad it would have been to hear them cry back for their father.

Of course, I don't blame Betsy for leaving. When a man cannot provide for his wife and family, then the wife has no obligation to stay. There were arguments beforehand, of course. Betsy was adamant I shouldn't have taken the pistol to work with me in the first place. Bless her, she had no understanding of the cut and thrust of business in the City. 'My dear,' I would say to her, gently taking her hand, 'your innocence is beguiling but sadly misplaced. I work with men of principle. They simply will not react to schoolboy postulations and hyperbole. They respect action, and action alone.'

She merely sighed and returned to her embroidery. Her reactions were no more aureate when I returned to tell her of my dismissal. It was almost as if she suspected it. 'My dear,' I said stoutly, 'I have news.' And I told her of how I had shook up those swine on the board of directors, and how I had subsequently been wrestled to the ground by a member the constabulary and escorted from the premises. The Bank's treatment of me, in the matter of a mere few thousand pounds' loss, justified ramifications of an equally dramatic nature. When they failed to understand that a man of my standing had the right to a privileged lifestyle, I was forced to unsheath my pistol, in order to demonstrate the seriousness of my fiscal mutability. I had, after all, sacrificed much of my life for my work and had little to show for it. But placing their lives in immediate danger failed to convince them of my need for solvency; instead of rousing their sympathy for my situation, I had, in fact, unnerved them greatly, and sent many of them into fits of fright and trembling that would have shamed even a foreigner.

'What are we to do for funds?' she had asked. 'Fret not, my sweet,' I replied with gusto. 'When I left, I left with such dignity and poise that many of the board were in tears. If anything, this turn of events has increased my standing in the circles of commerce, for a man who proudly abides by the consequences of his actions is a man both feared and respected.' 'Well,' she said, 'I hope you are both feared and respected when the bailiffs arrive.' Betsy had always held pretensions to wit.

These jolly ruminations of bygone days were curtailed by a sharp rumbling deep within my bowels. I feared my hunger might soon have some adverse effect upon my reasoning, and craved a pipe to sharpen my thoughts. Patting my pockets, I realised with dismay that I must have left my pouch and briar on the mantel in the sitting room, where I had been reading before lunch. It is a sorry state of affairs when the only person you trust to go and fetch your comestibles has a bullet through his lung, and you must forego both food and tobacco. To make matters worse, my crystal decanters were set on the sideboard just out of arm's reach, so it seemed even a tipple was beyond my means. Starvation seemed a less pressing concern when the prospect of sobriety loomed even larger, and I felt my vexation rise.

'On your feet, man,' I hollered at the butler.

Though my mounting impatience was evident in my tone, he still refused to stir. 'Dash it, do you know the discomfort I'm in?' For the first time since his service began, I lamented never learning his name, since I now suspected he may have been ignoring me by boldly assuming I was addressing someone else. Seeing as his face was buried in the carpet, I had no way of reading his expression and confirming these suspicions. 'I have had the clap, scrofula and lost four toes to gangrene, and never did I neglect my responsibilities,' I said. Alas, no response was forthcoming. He remained sprawled, lacking even the dignity to respond. I made a mental note to lecture him on the value of civility at a later, more opportune moment. Seeing as I was wanting of companionship, I whistled for Nelson, my thoroughbred bloodhound. So superlative a specimen of the canine genus was not to be found anywhere in the surrounding environs. He was sharp as a tack and would always heed my call, but it seemed that even he had foresaken me in these disheartening times, for I had not seen him all day. It was most odd.

With nothing to eat, drink or smoke, I turned to my pistol for comfort. Were I to sit here for a fortnight with not a crumb to eat nor a drop to drink, I could still have found solace in my snub-nosed friend. Through all my recent tribulations, my pistol had not deserted me, never leaving for its mother's cottage or bluntly refusing to serve my lunch. Its comforting weight always sat neatly in the pocket of my coat, and often, during boring conversations at the Club or at those wretched dinner parties, I would slip my hand inside my jacket and lovingly caress the cool metal of the trigger and the warm, tender varnish of the stock. Call me a soft old goat if you will, but I had even taken to giving it a gentle kiss before bedtime. It had never rejected my affections.

I released the catch beneath the barrel and clicked the chamber open. There were still five bullets left. Satisfied, I pushed the drum back into its housing and twisted to ensure that it would not misfire. I looked around the room for a target. If nothing else, I could idle away my time with some much-needed target practice. I spotted a vase on the sideboard. It was a large, flowery affair containing an aspidistra, and was beloved by Betsy owing to the fact it was a gift from her mother on the occasion of our marriage. I shot it with tremendous glee, thrilled like a schoolboy by the big noise I made and the explosion of porcelain and soil. I must admit, however, a twinge of guilt for the plant, which had never done me any harm. I then shot Emily's teddy through the head, which delighted me, as I had always assumed I had no skill as a marksman. After that, I tried to shoot the lightswitch, curious as to the effect of a bullet upon electricity, but after two failed attempts, I became bored and put the gun back in my pocket with a sigh.

After four gunshots, the room was now filled with a foul-smelling smoke. My recent sigh had drawn much of this hazy fug into my lungs, causing a not inconsiderable bout of coughing. Composing myself, I once more cursed the butler for not being cognisant. The room desperately needed an airing and, ever since I pinched my fingers in a latch as a child, I have refused to open any window myself. But it seemed that my revolver was not the only source of smoke. Through the pestiferous stench of gunpowder I could clearly discern the subtler odour of burning meat. It seemed that my dinner had ignited; such carelessness on the part of my butler did not make me any more repentant for shooting him. In truth, I was annoyed that he was already shot, for this oversight was surely grounds for shooting him again.

As I reflected on this, it occurred to me that I had displayed considerable restraint in not putting a bullet through him sooner. Though he had been with us some time, he was not the most genial or dedicated retainer. I remember the day Betsy left, when he had come into the lounge and disturbed me during *Letters to the Editor*. 'Madam has left,' he informed me with a supercilious air, 'taking Master Ralph and Miss Emily with her.' Not looking up from my paper, I told him I was aware of this, for I had seen them getting into a cab through the window. 'I don't think sir understands,' he continued. 'Madam informed me she was leaving for good.'

'Blast it, you imbecile!' I said. 'Do you think she'd be leaving for *bad*? How dare you assume meaning in the actions of another man's wife!'

This was only one example of his insolence. I would often have to ring the service bell for upwards of ten minutes, and when he finally arrived he would treat whatever request I had as inconveniencing whatever humdrum routine he practiced below stairs, tutting and huffing when I asked him to perform as trivial a task as pouring me another glass of scotch. I often suspected he had ideas above his station, as on one occasion he even had the temerity to ask me when he would next be paid. 'Honest work is its own reward,' I replied, sagely. I often tendered him with such pearls of wisdom, and felt he would do well to take them to heart.

But the extent to which he abused his position, not to mention my own naturally magnanimous demeanour, was never reason enough for me to discharge him. Although I had not received guests for some time, had any of my acquaintances deigned to visit and, God forbid, discovered me tending to my own house like some scrabbling fishwife, I should never have been able to show my face in public again. It would not do well for a man of my standing to be seen without the requisites. To this end, I had devised a scheme that would ensure I was never without the necessary services of a butler. With everybody gone, I could hardly be expected to live alone, and any conversation I started with the dog proved fruitless. So one night, long after the valet had retired to his quarters, I made a foray around the house and locked every door that allowed passage to the outside world. The keys allowing egress I kept on my person at all times. Not only that, I glued every ground-floor window shut. Provisions, I instructed the grocer, were to be delivered every three days, and brought into the house by means of a basket attached to a pulley I had had installed on a window-sill on the second storey. I have to admit to a not inconsiderable pride in the ingenuity of this system, and at one stage even considered patenting it, until I realised I would have to abandon the house to do so. I was loathe to leave the butler to his own devices. Goodness knows what he would have achieved in my absence.

Initially, he had not reacted well to his incarceration, and complained of what he regarded as 'bizarre and inhumane treatment'. As he said this, I had produced my pistol and, in my sternest tone, reminded him how lucky he was to be working for me. Thankfully, this resolved the matter, and not another word was said about it.

That was nearly a fortnight ago. In the meantime, the butler had lost a lot of weight and become pale and withdrawn. On more than one occasion I had discovered him cowering beneath tables, often after I had been occupying the same room for up to an hour, unaware of his presence. He had also adopted the annoying habit of flinching whenever I addressed him. It was, in fact, one of these involuntary spasms that eventually led to my having to shoot him. He was serving me my soup when his inveterate trembling caused some of it to spill upon my person. Not only was I slightly scalded, the dress shirt I was wearing was the only one remaining to me, since no matter how many items of soiled clothing I left out for the butler to launder, none returned clean or pressed. 'By Jove, man,' I said, 'look at what you've done. 'I'm damned if you haven't ruined my best shirt.' As I said this, he dropped to his knees. So degrading a gesture of weakness filled me with immediate contempt, and I rose my hand to strike him.

'Forgive me, sir,' he uttered, voice tremulous. 'I haven't had sleep for these ten days past.'

'That's no fault of mine,' I said. 'You should drink some warm milk before bed, as I do. It's bad enough the house being filthy without you falling ill on my hands.'

'I do the best I can in the hours I have, sir,' he pleaded. 'But I have not eaten, either. There's no longer food enough for two. I am trying my best!'

'Trying my patience, more like,' I said, and I chuckled at this rather witty remark, before readopting a stricter expression, lest the butler assume I was attempting to befriend him. 'The soup is vile,' I remarked pointedly. 'It tastes as if it came straight out of a tin.'

'But the soup *is* tinned, sir. I found it at the back of the larder. We've had no delivery for nigh on a week, and the grocer's boy told me that until the bill is settled, he wasn't to bring us any more food.'

'Tinned soup?' I yelled, incensed. 'Am I to live out my days on the rations of a dosshouse? I have expectations! A man is a moulded thing, sir! A thing of iron! If I would not change myself for my wife, then why on earth should I change my eating habits for one such as you? A man cannot change, sir! You have overstepped the mark! Be gone from my sight!'

But when he rose and turned to leave it occurred to me that such abysmal behaviour should not go unpunished. A man of my calibre, hoodwinked into eating tinned soup? It was almost beyond reproach. But not quite. To teach him not to attempt such base dishonesty again, I pulled out my pistol and I shot him in the back.

After some minutes, finding I had nothing else to occupy my time, I begrudgingly ate the soup. I made every effort possible not to enjoy it.

And that, I suppose, brings me back to my current predicament, although now the room is filled with smoke and it appears there are flames on the stairs outside the dining room. I thought of Nelson, and wondered where he could have got to, for a dog as intelligent and loyal as he would surely have barked to alert his beloved master to danger. Perhaps he was punishing me. Though I heartily shun any feelings of remorse, my recent demands for food had been so great that little Nelson must have gone wanting. If I was to believe what the butler had told me, and that we were, indeed, out of food, then provisions for the dog must have seemed a somewhat costly indulgence. Perhaps in a rare moment of compassion, the butler had let my little Nelson free to forage in the outside world. Perhaps not. Either way, I hoped he had been spared the flames, for it would be a great indignity for a dog of his class to be roasted alive.

Oh, what a dreadful situation in which to find oneself, and, as if to make matters worse, to find oneself in it on a Tuesday. I always found Tuesdays so painfully dull. Even the pretty twinkling of the fire cannot hold my interest for more than the briefest of moments. I feel hungry and so terribly bored. I have even tired of looking at my pistol. If the worst comes to the worst, I suppose I could always use the blessèd contraption on myself. But there is time enough yet. Some distraction may yet arise and spirit my attention to pastures new. If my butler wasn't so indolent, he could have alerted the fire brigade, for it is getting terribly hot in here. How typical of him to neglect his duties at so critical a juncture. In the morning, I fear I shall have to fire the swine. For a man of my standing to burn to death is really quite, quite unthinkable.

Sins

RAGNAR ALMQVIST

We drove to the hospital, mam and myself, to see him, this man we did not know.

You could hardly tell he was alive to look at him. His eyelids twitched occasionally, that was all. Blond hair, he had, big broad shoulders and a hooked nose, though whether it had been like that before the accident or not I didn't know. Round the side of his jaw you could see an ugly clump of stitches, where he'd been cut. A fuzz of stubble, faintly strawberry, grew around the outskirts of this wound like moss round a jagged mountain rock. On the locker by the bed was a string of cards drawn in childish hand. Get Well Soon, Daddy. Smiling cats towering over lopsided houses. A man with hands longer than his legs. A car driven by a rabbit.

I stood over him. The pulse machine blipped.

'Poor man,' my mother said, then again, as if for emphasis, 'poor, poor man.'

But it was not him I was thinking of.

'Christ,' I whispered.

My mother nodded weakly.

I was sitting in the kitchen when the first call came. Her gasp was barely audible beneath the hissing of the kettle.

'Sorry,' she said, 'when did this happen?'

I turned from my egg and chips.

'Okay… you're quite sure?'

Her face was strained, deep wrinkles furrowing the base of her brow and a hard look to her mouth. I raised my eyebrows, but she looked through me, then cast her head down towards the floor.

'God,' she said, 'God', and shook herself. 'Where can we…? No, right away. Thank you.'

The receiver caught the edge of its holder as she replaced it and slipped down towards the floor, only not quite reaching. It hung there, feeding noiseless static into the quiet room.

'Mam,' I asked, 'is everything alright?'

'No,' she said, 'no it isn't.'

In the coffin, I imagined him fingering his watch, checking the time, thinking what a great joke this was, how they'd scream and laugh when he popped out like a zombie just as the first sods were slung. He loved practical jokes, jokes of any kind, but I had seen him in the morgue, I reminded myself, a sheet of metal wedged into his skull, his torso stiff and grey, and I knew that there was no joking here. He was dead, and, given everything, it was probably as well for him.

'…a hard worker,' the priest was saying up at the altar, his thin voice crackling out over the speakers, 'and a good man, well respected by all who knew him and much loved. Fifty-three years old, he leaves behind him three children, Seán, Norah, and Criostabhair, who miss him greatly, a loving wife, Síle, two brothers, Seán and…'

The priest's catalogue reminded me of those in prison movies, where a criminal's possessions are read out before him on committal, confiscated, and placed in some great steel drawer. Later the prisoner is released and collects these same belongings, finding amongst them a single stick of gum, which he chews deliberately as he steps out into free air, though it may be forty years old.

'…his cat, Tomás, whom he would sometimes call an t-Oileánach, the wry sense of humour he was famed for…'

My mother was wearing a dress she'd bought for her own father's funeral, not five years previous. She'd thickened out since then, her stomach pressing at the edges of the cloth where once it fitted snug. Her eyes seemed hard, as if all the grief had soaked out of them with that first night's tears. But I knew different.

When the time came, I rose and walked to the pulpit behind my brother and sister. The priest nodded to us as we stepped in line, cue-cards nervously in hand. My brother's voice filtered out in front of me down the long, half-empty hall.

'Let us pray for the dead, and for the families of those who have died this past year. That they may be welcomed into God's kingdom and take solace in His love. Lord hear us.'

Lord graciously hear us.

Then my sister – those long, deliberate pauses that characterized her speech, the indignation resplendent in her tone.

'Let us pray for the poor around the world, for those dying in India and Iraq, for the suffering innocents of Sudan. That God may be with them in their final hours on this earth and usher them into the next. Lord hear us.'

Lord graciously hear us.

I stepped forward and stared down at those who sat before me, sweating in black suits and dresses in the summer heat. Parched, my voice caught in my throat just as I pushed to speak, so that I was forced to cough, recompose and begin again.

'Let us pray for those who are ill and dying closer to home, and for forgiveness, that God may look on us with compassion and acknowledge that even the best among us have sinned, though we know it not ourselves.'

'You forgot the Lord hear us,' my sister whispered to me as we walked back down the aisle.

'Christ,' I said, 'you're right.'

When I was eight years old my father saved my life. It was down in Ventry. Sometimes the tide down there stretched so far out, you'd be tired just running from pier to water's edge, your bare feet clipping along the sand, harder and darker the closer you came to the sea. This day though, the waves had swallowed up the dunes, and were licking the rocks like they were lollypops. No wind to speak of, the sky was grey. My brother and I had our rods out and in the water. We'd no bait, but were hoping the hooks looked attractive enough on their own somehow. Twenty minutes at it and we had caught three spools of seaweed, which Seán took as a positive sign, though I was less optimistic. Our mouths tasted of salt. I could feel it in my spine even, tickling the hard bone.

Seán turned to me. 'D'you think we could use the seaweed as bait, hide the hook in it?'

I was shaking my head when the wave hit.

It seems to me, looking back on it, that what I experienced drowning was exactly what television suggested I would. My memories look like movie scenes – shots of water, darkness, rocks. An unsteady camera. The sea moaning. Some unidentifiable screams. My father's arm loops round me suddenly, a massive branch, drags me back to concrete. His face looks more gaunt at these moments, more detailed. He glares at me from above, water catching the ends of his beard, glistening. 'You're okay, Christy,' he shouts, 'you're okay.'

I found I couldn't sleep. I stayed awake until dawn some nights, watching sitcoms, smoking joints my brother had left me before he went, drinking through my father's whiskey. During the days I would fiddle around with his guitar, or head into town and have coffee with friends. My appetite was meagre and I ate little.

A friend asked me to come running with him and I agreed to. We turned inward as we ran, thinking, and then not. The concrete was our conversation, the thump of his feet answering mine. We sweated and gasped.

'Fucking hard work, isn't it?' he said, looking at me, as we stood in his front yard filling our mouths with water so cold it hurt to swallow.

'Yeah,' I replied, 'damn right.'

I did it every night I could. As summer rolled through autumn and into winter, the sweat from our bodies turned to steam. One night, I sprained an ankle, two miles from home, and had to walk the distance. Crowds of teenagers laughed as I hobbled along, their jeers cutting through the chill. When the swelling had subsided and the sprain healed, I suited up again and set out, only to find, a dozen strides in, that I had lost interest.

'Lost interest?' my friend said to me, scratching the base of his neck. 'How do you mean?'

I shrugged, looked back down the road, shrugged again.

'I think I'd like to speak to her.'

My mother turned to me. 'Who?' she asked.

'His wife.'

Her features clouded over momentarily. I bit my lip. 'What will you say?'

She folded her hands and held them to her face, covering her mouth and nose as if to stop the words escaping. I squinted at her but didn't answer right away.

'I'll know when I know,' I said eventually, not knowing at all.

The second call we had been expecting.

'Is this Mrs Byrne?' came the voice at the other end, quiet and confidential.

'Yes,' I said, quickly, 'no, I mean, sorry, I'm her son. Christy.'

'Christy.' There was a long pause followed by the sound of paper rustling. 'Right, my name is Sergeant Keegan. I'm from the Garda station down the road from you there. I've been working on your father, on the accident. We've – ' – he paused again – 'is your mother in by any chance?'

'No, she left a while ago, down to her sister's, I think.'

'Have you a contact number there, a mobile or anything?'

'She doesn't carry one. I could give you her sister's.'

'Do that so.'

I fumbled for my mobile, scrolled through the phone box and read out the number. He thanked me and offered his condolences.

'Can I ask what this is about, just in case, in case you can't reach her maybe?'

'Well,' he said, slowly, like he was reading off a rolling cue, 'I'd want to leave that to your mother. It would be up to her, I think, how it should be told.'

'Right,' I said, 'thank you.'

He hung up.

I didn't call her. Instead I ran, and, when I stopped running, I studied. In the months after Christmas I found within myself a willingness to work I had never hinted at before. I was in the final year of teacher training and the load was heavy. Yet the pressure under which we were placed seemed to liberate me from the tensions of ordinary living. My results were impressive and, thanks to that and some solid references, I was offered a position at a nearby primary.

I remember my father saying to me once, home from work himself, his hands raw and frosty, that a tired man is a happy man. 'How's that?' my mother shouted back from the cooker, where she was frying up our tea. Smiling, he replied, 'Well love, tired men don't think, do they?'

In October I had my first parents-teacher meeting proper. I sat in the empty classroom and looked at the pictures decorating the walls around me, images so colourful and amateurish they might have been drawn by professionals. Sunlight filtered through the half-shuttered windows. Chalk hung in the air, a thick and comforting smell.

I spoke with one parent at a time. We discussed their children in hushed tones, as if they were sacred objects.

Jamie is struggling with Irish.

Yes, she's a good little reader alright, but there are problems all the same.

No, not A.D.D., nothing so extreme.

It's just the dentist said he should drink at least one carton a day. Sometimes, yes, I suppose that would be okay.

If you could read with him, maybe – a little each night?

No, well, I'm not sure exactly why.

She's very intelligent, I know that, but she still needs to fit in.

His father is in a coma. That might explain –

'A coma,' I interrupted, looking at this woman opposite me with renewed interest. She was small and square with a pretty face, only gently made up.

'A car hit him.'

I scratched my ear, put my hand to my mouth and dropped it again.

'That is… difficult. My father –'

'Yes, it's –'

We looked at one another.

'Sorry, I interrupted –'

'No, not at all.'

'No, I did.'

She waved her hand in front of her face.'Please, you were saying?'

'I was just … that must be tough. I can't think how tough it must be, to lose a father, at his age.'

Her hazel eyes were set deep into a sallow face. My hands twitched.

She shrugged, breaking contact. 'Don't worry. I just, thought it might explain how Tom's been getting on, that's all.'

I nodded. 'Read to him,' I said, 'read with him, if you can, if you have the time.'

'I'll try,' she replied, stepping out the door.

'He'll be okay,' I assured her, 'he'll get by. I'll make sure he does.'

I stood silently for a moment by the half-shut door, absorbing the emptiness, trying not to think at all, just let the world wash through me.

My mother was sitting at the table drinking coffee from the giant teacup. Seán had given it to her as a gift one Christmas when we were young – won at a school fair along with a matching saucer, big as a dinner plate, which he gave dad. That had broken, dropped, I think. The cup I hadn't seen in a long while.

'I didn't hear you come in,' I said, flicking the kettle switch to on.

She nodded vacantly.

'Where'd you find the cup?'

'In a box of your father's things up the attic. I was rooting around there the other day, looking for some photos.'

'Yeah?'

'There was one taken in Brittany of you and Norah and Seán, all three of you holding great big baguettes, tall as yourselves. That and some others of your father and me.'

'Find them?'

'No,' she replied, letting her eyes linger on the steam spiralling up from the hot coffee, 'no, I didn't.'

'But you got the cup.'

The corners of her mouth turned up slightly. The kettle had boiled. I poured myself some tea and sat down beside her.

'The Guards phoned while you were out,' I said. 'I gave them Bríd's number. Did they get you there?'

She shook her head. 'What was it about, did they say?'

'They didn't. Just that they wanted to talk to you.'

She frowned towards the table.

'It was only a matter of when.'

Tom looked at me, eyes brown like his mother's, his face slight and reddening. A big splotch of blue ink was soaked deep into his trousers, just above the left-hand pocket.

'Tom,' I asked 'are you okay?'

'Yes,' he replied, then looked down at his hands. They were cut, slight nicks from the gravel where he'd tripped and fallen.

'Come on,' I said, 'we'll have to get you cleaned up.'

He followed me through the scrambling crowd of chasing children and into the school building. Rummaging around in the medical box, I found a bottle of Dettol, some cotton swabs, and a few small plasters. He was silent.

'You'll be alright Tom, don't worry.'

In the bathroom I told him to wash his hands and he did, staring at the reflection of disinfectant in the mirror, amber and pungent.

'Right,' I said, 'this might sting, but only for a second, okay?'

His eyes became small creases in his face and his mouth twitched but remained shut.

'There,' I said, ripping open a plaster and spreading it tight over the scrapes, 'that wasn't so bad, was it?'

I had heard these words as a child myself, delivered by a hundred different adults in a hundred different situations, and they had always struck me as meaningless, something people said to children when they had nothing else to say. Tom looked up at me, the way I had probably looked up at all those adults from my past, teachers, doctors, nurses, parents, and shook his head dutifully, his eyes dark like clouds threatening rain.

'No,' he said.

We stood there for a long moment, eyeing one another in the glass.

'You know my father was hurt in an accident, too,' I stumbled out, breaking the silence.

Tom's eyes turned towards me.

'These things happen,' I said, nodding.

He nodded back.

The first time I got drunk was in my father's company. We were down the pub at midnight, pints in hand.

'It's twelve,' he said, clapping my shoulder. 'You're a man now. Drink up.'

I took a slug, letting the malt slide over my tongue.

'How'd you like it? Taste the same now you're of age?' His voice was smooth, deep and strong.

'It tastes well enough,' I replied, thinking this to be a satisfactory answer to both questions.

'Just don't go telling your mother that,' he smiled, fiddling a cigarette from his pocket and lighting it. He took a deep drag and breathed out, letting the smoke seep from his nostrils down onto the table face. I shook my head and coughed.

'Last orders, please,' came the shout from the bar, followed by the jangling of a bell.

'Right,' my father said, standing up and smoothing down his trousers. 'One more for the road.'

I sat there beside my brother and let my eyes wander around the room. You could almost see the warmth of the place sweeping up from the wine carpet beneath you. Paintings of racehorses along the walls covered so thick with lacquer that they shone, and the seats big, plush, red things, which swamped you when you leant back into them. My brother beside me sipped at his pint, his eyes wide and glazy.

'Happy birthday then, young spooner,' he said. 'It's good to have another man in the family; takes some of the burden off of me.'

His voice was steady enough, though a touch harsher than usual. I smiled. 'You and your burden,' I said, shaking my head dismissively.

'I'm telling you,' he replied.

I drained the last of mine and rolled my head round my shoulders the way I'd seen cats do. It felt good, sitting there in the heat, thinking of the rain lashing down outside, and all the poor bastards caught under it.

My father came back with three pure-looking pints.

'A holy trinity,' he smiled, placing the triangle on the hard wood table and lifting them onto coasters one at a time. I went to take a sip of the one set nearest me.

'Hold on there, Christy,' my father said. 'You boys didn't think these pints were for you now did you? I always take three at close, sure you know that.'

He looked at me with such earnestness that for a moment I was fooled. Then my brother laughed, breaking the mood.

'Bastards,' I said, and took a gulp, smiling under the layers of cream and black, in spite of myself.

Twenty minutes later we had them finished.

'Right,' dad said, 'off we go so.'

Several men nodded us goodbyes as we stepped out the doors into the car park.

'Christ,' Sean said, 'cold, isn't it?'

My father and I nodded and shuffled towards the car, hands plunged deep in pockets. The windows were iced over. We wiped them down with our coatsleeves and sat inside, switching on the heater so as to let our blood thaw.

'Yep,' my father said, shaking his head, 'the roads are going to be a bitch.'

I nodded grimly in the backseat, rubbing my ears.

'Still, sooner gone, sooner home, eh boys?'

'No rest for the wicked,' Seán answered.

'A good night to turn eighteen,' my father said.

In the shadows thrown by the car park lights, my brother and I nodded. The click of our seatbelts into their holders was the sound pennies make when they fall against a hard stone floor.

What Ghost Burns

JENNIFER BRADY

What Ghost Burns

What bitter shadow's random sweep steals shade from
where I crouch to watch your gentle mouth speak daylight
to my corner of hiding? I bolt in your illumination, so
shiny, so horribly deserving, I lip-read monstrosities of
love. Fictions I create to make the light a little easier on
the eye that squints under your gaping sky of truth.
Your shine scorches, your flame, the ghost that burns a
weaker light away.

Sister

Long nights of giddiness and boredom through bunk-bed
slats in the room we hated sharing, and us with only one
more token of *I Scream, You Scream* left to keep us
together. Sometimes a mosaic would pass our way, or a set
of markers, or a rehearsal for a play. Landlocked sisters
are better than two on different islands. For all the fights, I
loved your succa-thumb, cradling your beady eye when I
pulled back the foam.

One-Man-Band

Grim gigs those pubs, those hotel bars, proprietors
counting on a croon to woo punters to the double gin and a
domestic later with the spouse when the taxi fails to show.
He plucks indifference with the forced zeal of a tap-
dancing monkey and prods the plus sign on the Casio
machine to ratchet up a tempo, cause a stir, so by anthem
time they'll be mouthing *The Soldiers' Song* in Irish and
buying another round. The programmed tracks bring tears
to my eyes: Lady in Red Ride On Friends in Low Places
have me buying him whiskey-chasers to ease the imaginary
cymbals off his knees.

Glib Realisation at the Politician's Dinner Party

So, you're an open book to choruses of 'not you', wine
glasses clinking as you chew the compliments of men who
can't resist the boyish charm of beardless face and women
too are pleased to note your bicep flexing in their hold –
a teenage son whom they adored, one mother could have
nurtured more? But open book of deprecation, penned by
self, by implication the grooming of a lover's tongue is
never really that much fun, it drives the appetite of need,
resentful, drunk, in love, in greed, to scream through smile
and stifled snore *if this is it then I want more.*
Such loyalties to man and vote, batter shapes in docile
moulds, like admiring cufflinks and aftershave, correctly
smelt and well behaved.

Cocoa Barter

Clear soup cleans a greedy stomach that has finally
registered the reality of loving. Sharing flat tyres and
broken steering, driving off kilter, in need of a mechanic
again, and the cycle to work – see you later! Kiss, one
cheek, kiss, the other, perishing on the way back home,
weeds choking the garden, money down drain, impending
seeking of remortgage, impending repayment increase,
improvements outside and inside the gutter of domesticity:
a grater on a chopping board, a lemon slashed, cuticles
stinging on evening's stretched-out sofa, companionable
legs racked up like burdensome flatmates' feet on a coffee
table, citrus setting in – one a news-watcher, the other
wants a soap. In the kitchen, soup-dishes still undone.
Tantrums threaten – you go to the shop, no you, or else:
a crossword at a bar, a pub somewhere in town, the
comfort of a stranger, a party till dawn. Stalemate.
Chocolate now, or tomorrow you dine alone.

Confession

Your hand bending the hem, loving her rigidly, uneasy stranger, thrilled sick by deceit, feigning after the posture of sleep, mentally chalking around your enjoyment like an accident. Didn't she hear your half-hearted singing as you sweetened the sweat of foreign skin made sour and milky with soap?

Warning on Eve of

Stake claim, skull jury, stake claim. Creep carefully dim cracks of
craggy tombs, vacate this pool of blood and heat and lie in
unkempt plots, half-in-half-out till dawn. Unsteady
skeleton: be the sculpture that once dragged the heart behind, be
the bone chipped bare before flesh chalked on fact and
wallowed in easy vinegar while the city crumbled and
proved you right. Stake claim, skull jury. Reach down to
that sluggish aorta and squeeze it firmly in your hand.

Snow after Istanbul

Bath hot, white, foaming bubbles and the bubble bath itself
milky. I lie under water, shifting darkness – I sink, I soak the last
of the Near East away. I can only go from here, let dirt loose
and emerge the way I could if I started again, all over again.
Concrete routines evolve. This track back again, Bosphorus
dreams retreat. Working a day down, another full day of earning.
But today, wheels print crisply my cycle to work, and above,
bulging hammocks are stuffed with fluff-flakes, resting and
swaying, resting and swaying. Tip them over. I hope the wool
falls white all day and the industrial park lies bright and
blanketed, its necessary routes silent, sleepy, undriven.

I Loathe You, Too

LUKE ANDERSON

Lily says it's a way of lookin' at the world. Like everything that is and was can just be up and forgotten. Lily says it's not so bad, because the way we've always done things ain't always been the easy way. She says someday things'll be different and we'll have beautiful babies and call them Carlo and Sophia or some other names that don't sound so much like the places we been. Most nights I lay awake and stare upwards through the blackness, wonderin' when things'll be different, if we can set ourselves right and if I'll make a good daddy. Lily's always talkin' on how someday I'll make a good daddy, but someday is long ways comin' and so we're still here, in the city, trying to find our way back out and into the world. Lily says she doesn't mind havin' a little place, but I want something big, a big house tucked beneath a mountain and maybe beside a river. Lily says it's just dreams. We been here only three weeks so I figure I'm still allowed to dream and think on how much fun it was supposed to be – how easy it were gonna be with just me and Lily and the city.

Most Sundays we just sit inside and read over them papers, tryin' to find me or Lily a better job, something at least to pay for the air conditionin', or maybe something so we can put a little away. But it's August and without that air the thick heat just soaks through them walls so by noon were about soaked and want nothin' more than to kick off for the rest of the day and go swimmin'. I tell Lily about the quarries. I tell her how cold and black that water is and how good it feels when it's hot like today. Lily puts down her paper and looks up at me and the sweat's curlin' down off her face but she don't seem to notice.

'Swimmin'?' she says, 'We cain't go swimmin'. We've gotta find you better work.' Lily takes her paper and puts it back up to her face and keeps reading without wiping that sweat from her forehead.

'There ain't no work,' I say. 'There ain't no work better than what I got,' but the truth is there's a lot better places to work if they would only take me on. There's places that ain't so hard and still pay more, so maybe we could afford things like air conditionin', even if it's just for every now and then. Days like today it ain't right to not have that air.

Lily doesn't answer, just keeps reading and lettin' that sweat run down her face and pretendin' like she don't notice or care. When the paper's done it's almost two and my shirt's off and my shorts is off and I'm just standin' there in the room in my drawers tryin' my best to keep cool.

'Come on, Lily,' I say. 'It's too dern hot to be just sittin' here sweatin'. Let's go down to them quarries.'

Lily fans herself with her paper and looks up at me standin' there sufferin' in nothing but my drawers. She smiles, even laughs a little, and keeps on fanning.

'How we gonna get down to Schuyler without any gas money?' she says, 'Did you think about that? We sure ain't walkin', not in this heat.'

'I got ten dollars there in my pocket,' I say, and reach to fetch it out.

'Where did you get ten dollars?' Lily says, standin' up, lookin' like I stole it or something.

'From tips, Lil,' I say, holdin' the bill up, 'I got it from tips.' And Lily relaxes a little but doesn't sit down.

'We better save it then,' she says. 'Put it in the jar, we can't be wastin' it on swimmin',' and my head drops but I hold on to that money without puttin' it in the jar or back in my pocket. Then I sit down and Lily sits down. The sweat's drippin' off her now and into her shirt and I'm lookin' at that ten dollars and it's startin' to look and smell a lot like water.

'It don't make no difference,' I say, 'ten dollars, twenty dollars – a *hundred* dollars,' but Lily don't say nothin', just keeps on fannin' and drippin'. Finally I just look up at her and hold that ten dollars and say, 'Please, Lil' and she sets down her paper fan and stares at me and smiles. For a second she's lookin' at me the way she used to look at me, like she's a second away from sayin' 'I love you' but hasn't quite got the nerve up yet.

'Please,' I say again, and I know she can smell that water so I hold the ten dollars a little higher and give it a little shake and Lily nods and runs and grabs our suits. Then we're out the door, drivin' south through the thick heat towards them quarries.

It's twenty miles to Schuyler and we need gas so we stop and I fill up the tank while Lily goes inside with the ten. Then we're back on the road and the truck's rattlin' something mighty, the whole time soundin' like it's gonna bust and just fall to pieces right there on the highway. Lily rolls down her window and lets her hair blow back in the wind. She sticks her hand out and flies it for a while, and suddenly I'm rememberin' the early days, when we were happy and everything was easy – when we'd drive for hours just to be out on the road and because we didn't have nothin' else to spend the money on. I'm rememberin' the first time we went swimming together – how it was hot and we snuck off to the lake and just laid out by that water all afternoon. Then suddenly while I'm drivin' that rattle-box truck I'm wishin' I was still out by that lake with just Lily and nothing else.

When we get up to speed the truck stops rattlin', or maybe just the wind outside is loud enough to drown out the rattlin', and we cruise down that highway for fifteen minutes and then take a left towards Schuyler. Lily ain't never seen the quarries and she's full of questions, askin' how come the quarries is there and how come there's water in them. So I tell her about the drilling and the blasting and say it started in the Depression even though I'm not really sure. Truth is, 'round here most big things like that started during the Depression, so why not the quarries too? Then I tell her about how them diggers suddenly hit a spring and the whole thing started fillin' up real quick like with that black water. Lily gets a start when I tell her that some men and most of the big equipment – trucks, cranes, and drills – got stuck and left behind and that they're still down there, beneath that water. Lily doesn't believe me about the men, so I tell her about the navy divers who came in a few years back to fetch them out, only the divers found the trucks and drills and cranes and not the men. I can tell that don't make Lily feel no better, so even though it's true I don't tell her that they also found catfish at least six feet long down there too.

Lily's quiet the rest of the way and I can tell she's thinkin' about them diggers, all old and soggy and trapped down there in that black water. I can tell she's wonderin' what they look like, and if they're really all dead or if just maybe they might pop up and grab her if she goes too deep. Or maybe she's wonderin' if those diggers really ain't down there, then maybe they've turned ghost and are runnin' around them quarries like a bunch of haunts and spooks.

Then finally we're there and I pull off the road into the dirt and park the truck and give it a pat to say 'thanks for makin' it', and grab our stuff and start into the woods. Lily takes a look around at where we are and says, 'You sure you know what yer doing?'

'Yes'm,' I say. 'We got to walk through them trees a little bit,' and I can tell she's a little nervous, like maybe I brought her out here for something other than swimmin', so I says, 'Quit fussin', the quarry's right through there,' but I don't think it helps none.

I start off through the trees and Lily follows, pickin' her way through careful like, so's not to touch anything green. First we're on a dirt road, and beside the road is all sorts of trash, even things like old stoves and washers, but mostly tires and heaps of junk. Lily's lookin' at it like maybe this was a bad idea, but she don't say nothin'. Then we turn off the road onto a smaller path and start downhill towards the quarries. Lily says somethin' about spiders, and how she's heard of some spiders that just drop right down out the trees and into your shirt. I ain't never heard of no spider that did that, but the cobwebs on the trail is buggin' me something awful, so I pick up a big ole stick and start wavin' it in front of me, catchin' all them cobwebs. Before too long we're at the drop-off down to the quarries.

Then we can see the water. The trail opens through the trees and we can see down into the quarries. Lily sees how far down it is and gets a start and says, 'How did you find this place?' and I think hard about it and really can't remember but say, 'Dirk showed me,' even though it's not entirely true, though it might be. Then I start climbin' down to the cliffs. The trail is worn back and instead of a path that levels out onto the cliffs there's a drop-off down to them, so's you have to climb. I go first, using roots and trees to help me down, and then Lily tosses down the suits and towel. Then I show her where to grab and where to put her feet so's not to fall and she makes it down alright, though not without a little cussin'. She asks me if we're trespassin' and still looks nervous so I tell her, 'No, we ain't', even though I'm not really sure. We walk out onto the cliffs and Lily grabs my arm when I get close to the edge.

The quarries form a big square where three of the walls are straight down and the fourth one is collapsed low enough so you can climb back out. All over the walls is drill marks and blast marks from where the diggers started in on that stone. About sixty feet down is the water – that cold black water. At the top the cliff where we're standin' the rock is flat and Lily peers over the edge wonderin' if she can see down to the bottom where those diggers are. But the water's so dark you can't see but five feet under the surface so Lily pulls back and says, 'How we supposed to get down?' and I look at her to see if she's serious and she is.

'Jump,' I say, and she laughs and shakes her head and says,

'No really, how we supposed to get down?' and I look at her again and say, 'Really, Lil, you gotta jump', and Lily gets one of those looks on her face like this really was a bad idea and she's thinkin' that maybe we shouldn't have spent that ten dollars.

'You're not jumpin' off that thing,' Lily says. 'You'll kill yourself. You can't even swim that good – how deep is it? What about them bodies?'

'I can too,' I says, 'we didn't come all this way out here just to sit, it's at least two-hundred foot. There ain't no bodies down there, Lil.'

Then I set the towel down on the rock and strip off my clothes to put my suit on and the whole time Lily's just watchin' me and smilin'. When my suit's on I sit down on the ledge and dangle my feet off the edge and Lily sits next to me but not so near the edge and leans into me, just holdin' her suit and not putting it on. For a while we just sit there, not really thinkin' about nothin', just lookin' out over the gray rock and black water of the quarry, 'cause it really is beautiful.

'Do you think we'll make it?' Lily says, and I say, 'It's really not that far, Lil, people swim and jump here all the time. You ain't gotta worry about them bodies.'

'No,' she says, 'not jumpin'. I mean you and me.' And I think for a second and look out over all that water and rock and listen to the big silence of the woods.

'We made it this far,' I say. 'I reckon we can make it farther', and Lily smiles and holds tight on my arm while the whole time I'm thinkin' can we really and truly make it, after all we've been through? Then Lily gives a little laugh and says, 'I loathe you', the way we used to say when we was too scared or nervous to say 'love', even though we always meant love. Then I take Lily's hand and hold it up to my face and give it a quick peck before pushin' off. Lily gets a start and I yell something back at her but can't really make it out over the rush of the air past my ears. For a second there's nothing but the pull of the wind. Everything that is and was just drops away, and for that quick second all the questions that don't have answers don't seem so important. Then there's the hard smack of the water and I'm twenty feet down, cold and stinging, lookin' up through the blackness at the sunshine and the rock.

Chuck

MEGAN PASLAWSKI

Pam never used the rubber gloves with Kimmy. She had taken the checklist to Pharmaprix a year ago and bought each item on it, but when the time came on Kimmy, all she could remember was the first night they were together. Kimmy had pushed Pam down on the bed, pressing with a mouth sour with Sleeman's lager, breathing with her stolen breath.

Pam had still planned to call it a mistake, just as soon as she'd named the taste on Kimmy's tongue, but then Kimmy had slid her bare fingers into Pam's cunt. It had been the naturalness that had got Pam, the way their thighs touched roundly. It had been the way they were naked together, without the fumbling for spermicides or shrink-wrapped condoms that you had with men.

Pam hoisted Kimmy onto the bed, squaring her hips with the disposable plastic and cotton square Pam had put down to protect the sheets. 'It's called a chuck,' the nurse had told her. 'Cause you can chuck it.'

Kimmy waved her hand. 'I'm afraid it's rather a mess in there.'

'Hm.' Pam popped the tape on the right side of the undergarment and rolled Kimmy over to get the left. 'I'd be more excited if you could manage another color every once in awhile. It gets boring.'

'We could eat more beets, I guess.'

She slipped the undergarment away from Kimmy, wrapped it in on itself, and tossed it into the pail. 'Only if you're the one who boils them.' She wiped Kimmy down and put a new undergarment on her, all without a smudge. She really didn't need the chuck at this point, but it was all part of the ritual.

Kimmy smiled, looking up at Pam's face. Pam crawled onto the bed, pressing her face between Kimmy's breasts, leaving Kimmy's yoga pants around her ankles. Kimmy struggled to bring her hand to Pam's head and stroke her hair. 'I love you,' she said.

'Mmm.' Pam blew a raspberry against Kimmy's skin. 'I love your breasts.'

'Dyke.'

Pam giggled because it was true, and she had once never imagined it would be. They lay like that for a long time, Pam mumbling in contentment, until it dawned on her to turn out the lights and fix Kimmy's pajamas. 'This is the best part of the day,' Pam sighed.

Kimmy twitched an arm onto Pam's stomach, tracing the stretch-marks with her fingertips, finding her groove even in the dark. 'I know, baby.'

Pam rolled over, stretching out her legs. 'You comfy?'

'Yup. I'd tell you.'

'Damn straight.' They both laughed.

Kimmy's fingers stopped, then drummed against Pam. 'Speaking of straight...'

Pam spoke into Kimmy's arm. 'Yeah?'

'I caught your son watching *Showgirls* this afternoon.'

'That boy.' Pam tried not to laugh. 'I hope he was as disappointed as we were.'

Kimmy's voice shook. 'Parts of him ... looked interested.'

'Oh my god.' Pam groaned into the darkness, remembering the mountains of stained sheets and stiff tissues. It was only in the past year he'd begun cleaning up after himself.

Kimmy was amused at Tim's expense. 'It's not like I could really say "don't watch my porn, kid". I told him I thought Kyle McLachlan's acting was good, really underrated, and I was glad he was a Canadian.

Then I left.'

'Glad he was a Canadian?' Pam couldn't even say the words without snickering. Tim didn't understand Kimmy's deadpan humor, not the way Pam did. He probably thought she meant it, probably thought thespian went with lesbian as well as it sounded. 'God, I'm glad he's eighteen now. I can't even begin to imagine how I'd bring that up, let alone scold him for it.'

'*I'm* glad he's eighteen now.' Kimmy's hand closed around Pam's breast. 'The wicked stepmother will have you alone at last.'

In two weeks, Tim would start at McGill University. It was only downtown, but since trains from the West Island took forever and no teenager wanted to live at home, they'd all agreed that he'd live in rez to get the full university experience. There was enough money from the accident settlement; they didn't need to be frugal.

'He'll be back. Probably when we're planning on making love in the living room.' Pam held Kimmy tighter then, thinking of how she still went down on her, even though Kimmy couldn't feel it when Pam touched her below the waist. Kimmy puckered her lips and Pam leaned over for a kiss. She tasted the takeout Thai they'd shared over the new episode of *Six Feet Under*, a favorite treat to go along with their favorite show.

Kimmy slept first, mouth open, and Pam made herself breathe in time. She fell into a slumber that deepened, resting her for tomorrow.

Tim could hear every word they were saying. It was like Mom didn't know that the walls were as thin as Kimmy looked next to Mom's bulk. It was like she didn't realize his favorite spot to sit had always been on the living room's wingtip chair, which backed onto her bedroom. Mom and Kimmy's bedroom.

Tim didn't mind that Mom had become a lesbian, especially since he'd had five years to get used to it. He did mind that the apartment always smelled like diapers, and that Kimmy left ashtrays at low levels so she could reach them and Tim could bump against them, spilling cigarettes onto the carpet. Mom hated it when he did that. The only real loss, though, was that this had made girl-on-girl porn endlessly gross to him.

He'd visited Grandpa earlier today. At first, the visits had been because someone had to do it and Mom's hands were too full with Kimmy. It turned out that Grandpa had good stories about World War II and packs of Belmont Milds to share. So, it was good that Mom had picked the nursing home next to Tim's school. Grandpa didn't think so, though. He'd been on about it again today.

'I'm only eighty-one years old.' Grandpa had lit two cigarettes and handed one to Tim. They had inhaled at the same time, holding in the smoke. Tim had needed to breathe out first. 'I don't need to be here.'

'Yeah,' Tim had said. Eighty-one was old, but Grandpa was fine. Mom just didn't want to worry about driving him everywhere now that his eyesight wasn't so good. 'I mean, you can walk. If anyone should be here, it's Kimmy.'

Grandpa had blown a smoke ring, which Tim still couldn't do. 'It's not my place to say anything. But it is true that she takes more of your mother's time than I ever would.'

'Wanna come to dinner tomorrow?' Grandpa hadn't been to see Mom in a while.

Grandpa had looked around his bachelor flat. 'If it's all right with Pamela.' He had gotten up to straighten the picture of Grandma, bumping his hip on the long table that had fitted in his old house. Here it just emphasized how cramped his room was. It was like Mom had put Grandpa in student housing.

Mom hadn't looked overjoyed. 'You'll have to help me make dinner. You think he'd want pork chops again?'

Tim had shrugged. 'Like anyone wouldn't want pork chops.' Other than Kimmy.

Mom had rested a hand on Kimmy's shoulder. 'I'll make some extra noodles for you.'

Tim stood up, stretching. There was nothing on TV, so he might as well go to bed. Passing their door, he decided not to say goodnight.

Pam didn't miss working at the *Régie du logement*. She'd heard enough 'terrible landlord' stories to last her a lifetime. She had enough to fill her time, and she liked having whole days to spend with Kimmy. She pulled Tim's clothes out of the dryer, pressing his *Canadiens* hoodie to her nose to smell the Mountain Fresh detergent. She added it to the stack on Kimmy's lap. Kimmy reversed out of the laundry room, bringing the clean clothes to Tim's room. Pam tore open the packaging on the sheets she'd bought for his new room in rez. They were softer when they were washed before use and God knows that Tim wouldn't do it. Then she joined Kimmy. 'Well.' She surveyed the room. 'It'll be nice not to worry about fungus growing in here anymore.'

Kimmy bumped her footrest against Tim's desk. A half-full coffee mug clattered against a bowl stuck with bits of Kraft Dinner. 'Bets on how long they've been there?'

Pam just sighed, stopping herself from sitting on the bed.

'So, how long before we can turn this into a guest bedroom?'

'Kim!'

Kimmy winked at her.

Pam had to laugh. 'I'm not saying that the thought hadn't crossed my mind.' She nodded at the *Sin City* poster over the desk. It featured a glowing blonde stripper, gyrating under the caption '*Skinny little Nancy Callahan. She grew up. She filled out.*' 'I've been dying to get rid of that. Makes me look like a bad Mom.'

Kimmy studied Nancy Callahan. Then she turned her scrutiny to Pam. She wrinkled her forehead. 'You look pretty good to me.'

Pam ruffled Kimmy's hair. 'I want to keep the room how it is for now, at least. I think it'll make the transition easier for all of us.'

'Makes sense.' Kimmy looked at the pile of stuff that needed to be packed still. 'Did you get him a roll of quarters for the laundromat?'

Pam added it to the list.

Tim swung by Grandpa's more than two hours before dinner. He'd brought a movie that Grandpa would probably like.

'You know, Clint Eastwood directed it?'

Grandpa handed Tim a whiskey and soda. 'I remember when he was just happy to do cowboy movies. But there's a lady boxer in this one?'

Tim raised his glass. 'Yeah. You'll like it.'

'Cheers.' They drank. Tim pressed *Play*.

Grandpa did like the movie. Tim could tell because he sat up during the ending, stopped rubbing his arthritic knee so he could fold his hands tightly in his lap. Tim liked the movie, too. He'd seen it three times already, and every time it took his breath away when Hilary Swank begged to be shot. It seemed so right to refuse a crippled life.

The end music played and the credits rolled, freeing Grandpa to shift in his old armchair. He cleared his throat. 'It's good to have a dignified death like that.' He lit another cigarette. 'When I was your age, I used to pray that I wouldn't get blown up or captured by the Japs or whatever.'

Tim nodded. He'd seen the medals Grandpa had kept, the telegram telling the death of his brother at Calais, but it only seemed real to him when Grandpa drifted off like this, half-talking to Tim and half to the army buddies he still sent letters to. 'But at least I'd have died with my boots on, felt alive beforehand. Better than slowly breaking apart, lying in bed with all the dead pieces of me.'

They sat together, thinking, stubbing out cigarettes in the ashtray that sat between them. Finally, they were ready for dinner with Pam and Kimmy. Tim watched his grandfather pick a path through the parking lot. His back was straight and his pace slow, clothes looking dry-cleaned. He looked like the old war hero he was. Tim opened Grandpa's door first, as if he was on a date with a girl who didn't think chivalry was dead.

'Onward, boy-o. To the women.' Grandpa buckled his seatbelt.

It'd be nice if Tim had rung the doorbell, just to give her one last second to get her game face on, but of course that wouldn't occur to a kid. Pam handed Kimmy the bottles of Jack and Coke so she could pour it out in the living room, giving the peas time to boil. Then she checked her face in the bathroom mirror, tweezers in hand, just in case she'd sprouted a chin hair. Not that Dad would be able to see it these days anyway, but it was bad enough for an old man that she had her female lover offering him drinks. She had better get in there.

'Chrétien had peaked politically, of course.' Dad held his glass up to the light filtering in from the bay window. 'Really the best thing that he quit when he did.'

Kimmy coughed. 'Some of his most important legislation happened that year.' She swatted Tim's hand away from the whiskey bottle.

'Such as decriminalizing drugs?' Dad sipped at his drink, frowning. He set it on the end table.

'If anyone needed medicinal marijuana, that guy did.' Tim let the left side of his face droop, wrinkling up his opposite eyebrow.

Kimmy bit her lip. Then she opened her mouth.

'Right!' Pam gestured towards the doorway. 'Dinner's ready.'

Kimmy hung back, letting Tim and Dad go first. Pam shrugged at her. It wasn't like Jean Chrétien's legacy was worth an intergenerational war.

Pam served the pork chops. 'Apple sauce, anyone?'

Dad's head was bent and his eyes were closed. His lips moved silently while Kimmy and Tim said 'no.' Tim then saw the praying, bowing his head in time for the blessing's end. Kimmy put some butter on her mashed potatoes.

'Apple sauce.' Pam handed the jar to Dad. 'So, who won poker this week?'

Dad trimmed a bump of fat off his chop. 'We haven't tallied it yet. Jerry's daughter was visiting.'

'Which one?' Kimmy had spent a cigarette break bitching about the nursing home staff with one of the daughters in question, and she remembered her fondly. Sometimes, Pam wished that she smoked too. 'Amanda?'

'No, Heather.' Dad chewed one hundred times before he swallowed. 'The one from North Bay. Though she seems to come around more often than Amanda.'

Pam tried to remember the family tree and map. 'Amanda's over in Ottawa, right? She's probably in all the time and you just don't realize it.'

Dad lined up his knife with the edge of his plate. 'It's very easy to put someone away and then forget all about him.'

'Yeah.' Tim stabbed another piece of meat off the center plate. 'Yeah.'

Maybe Pam hadn't cooked the peas long enough. They were a little harder than she would like. 'Oh c'mon, Dad. Amanda's a nice girl. Maybe she's just been busy recently.'

Kimmy sighed and had some more noodles. Pam passed her the parmesan cheese.

Tim put his milk glass down on the table too hard. It sloshed over, spilling on the mashed potatoes. Pam reached for the bowl too late; the potatoes lay sodden and looking dirty under the whiter milk. 'You can't just "get busy." People have responsibilities!'

'Yeah, like not ruining the potatoes.' Kimmy took the bowl and one-handedly shook its contents into the trash. 'Sorry, Archie. Hope you didn't want seconds.'

'Tim's right.' Dad looked at him, pale-pink lips twitching into a smile.

Pam bit her lip. Tim couldn't even do his own laundry. Wait until he'd been at university for a few weeks, then they'd talk about responsibility. 'Well, yeah. But Amanda does have that government job.'

'Family comes first.' Tim tilted his glass at Dad as though he were drinking his grandfather's health.

Kimmy took Pam's hand under the table. 'That's enough. Pam of all people doesn't need a lecture about family loyalty. She goes above and beyond.'

Tim stared at his plate. 'For you, maybe.'

'Oh, for god's sake.' Pam had thought he had grown out of that morose teenager crap. 'Tim, stop ruining dinner.'

'I think you should let the boy express his feelings.'

Pam looked up. This was new. Dad hadn't kept a copy of *Doctor Spock* around when she was growing up. 'Dad, I — '

'Stay out of it, Archie.' Kimmy was unstoppable now. 'Tim, give your mother a break, will you?'

'I'm not the one who needs her to wipe my ass.'

Dad's teeth parted a little. Kimmy stared across the table, eyebrows knitted with all the anger Pam knew she could feel. She reversed her chair, backing up into the hallway. Those left at the table heard her slam into the bedroom door to shut it.

'I cannot believe you.' Pam pushed away from the table and dumped her plate in the sink. 'I cannot believe you said that.'

Dad stood up. He picked up the salt and pepper, carrying them to the cabinet where they were kept a year ago.

'They go under the sink now, so Kimmy can reach them. You know that.' For a second Pam wondered if Dad had put Tim up to this outburst, but when he went into the bathroom she knew he was just an old man with prostate troubles.

Tim sat at the table.

Pam cleared her throat. 'You're going to apologize to Kimmy.'

'No.' He picked up his butter knife, balancing its weight against his palm.

'Tim, you can't just sulk until you leave for school. You've got to apologize. You owe it to her.'

He dropped the knife, banging it against the plate, but his expression didn't change.

Pam looked at him, trying to find the son she'd raised, but he turned his face away. This boy was sullen. He thought about strippers who grew up and filled out and danced for him. He had sat in her house, resenting her, wanting more from her than she could give. 'Pack your stuff, if you can manage to do it on your own. You're moving into McGill early, when the international students do, if you can't apologize.'

'You've just been dying to kick me out, haven't you?' Tim got up, knocking his chair backwards. 'So you and Kimmy can play Love Hospital.'

This was the little boy who had fallen out of his stroller, pounding his feet on the floor, holding his breath until his face turned blue. This was the pre-teen who threw a basketball into his friend's face.

'I mean it,' Pam said. She stopped in the doorway. 'Drive Grandpa back home.' She went into her bedroom.

Kimmy had managed to fling herself onto the bed. It took a lot of strain and wriggling, and she usually waited for Pam to help her. She looked up when Pam came in. 'I hope you realize I'm not going to kill myself for the good of the family.'

There was such a thing as humor that was too black. Pam sank onto the bed. She had to change Kimmy before they fell asleep, but it could wait a few minutes while they pushed the memory of dinner away. 'I'll make him move out early.'

Kimmy was silent. Pam came closer, bending her body around Kimmy's like a sling. Pam nearly let herself doze.

The car pulled into the driveway, sounding too fast, and the front door slammed. Pam held her breath to hear what Tim would do next. The opening music to *Million Dollar Baby* blared through speakers too old to process it so loudly.

'Jesus.' Kimmy had her back to Pam still.

Pam heaved herself up. She got the wipes, A&D ointment, and a fresh undergarment. She never used the rubber gloves with Kimmy, even if it did mean she got shit all over her hands.

Poems

KEITH PAYNE

Aubade

The state of her body writhing
Leaves no wonder any more

If only there was some mystery left
My warped adulteress.

Árainn

At twenty-nine the umbilical cord was cut,
it trailed away on the tail of the Queen of Aran
as I slipped down from the wall at Joe Mac's.

Unbuttoned, the fisherman continued his watery tales
for pony-trapped tourists eager to believe;
there's where Hy Brasil appears every one in six.

His weathered face took the sun like butterscotch
or milky tea he slurped over his breakfast
gazing past the granite erratics in his garden.

By lobster catch he predicts the weather;
they'll pack the pots when there's a squall coming in
and the men know not to venture out.

Each line of his face a trellised rope-pull
and hands that clamped the briny nets
now smooth the leather of his harness.

*Three turns of the stone will make a wall
that stands three thousand years*
around these undulating potato drills by the sea.

Sacred Heart

If we arrived early, I got to see her pink forearms knead the dough
And hear the nail scrape on the plastic mixing bowl
Range round with the rhythmic clang of her copper bracelet;
Behold the handmaid of the Lord.

When she turned to the sink, we prised toasted almonds
From the top of the fruit cake cooling on the sideboard,
Her scapular threads peeking from the scullery;
Pray for us, O Holy Mother of God.

The static pips from the wireless belonged there
With Frawleys, Thomas Street and the venous cod's roe from Stumpf's
Laid plump on the floured board;
And the Angel of the Lord declared unto Mary.

Her domestic stations done, she sat to the noon bells
And lipped her whispering prayers,
Her muscular fingers reading the Lourdes beads;
That we may be made worthy of the promise of God.

Kali

The titanic outstretched arms of Poll thoir an Dúin
Expose the island's body,
A hull of stratified rock, ghost grey
Thrust into green.
Wave breaks loosen the layers and backwash
Sucking at every crevice

Drawing the land to her
A crazed wench incessantly dancing
Thrashing on his stentorian chest
Then soft, each wave lapping a lover's caress.
She rails against her lover and seduces him to her bed.
He is urged forward and down
Down into her capacious mouth.
He cannot resist her leeching, he embraces all that he is not.

The Water Hurdle

Always I find myself at ease in the water
Where I hold the ridge of the boat
It chills my legs to float
So I don't let go. I cannot tell you
But hope in silence for more.
Darkness is distant, circling,
I am learning to breathe in the sea.

Marché

In the sun we bunched fresh thyme and basilicum,
Our gaze skirting the stain
At the apple crate.

Husked corn lay drilled in wicker baskets
Amid Chrysanthemums and Irish Eyes
Water dipped to salve the brutal heat.

The shorn beards of hanging garlic
Gathered ants
On the worn cobbles.

We shunted the sighing van with earthy potatoes;
Pommes de terre for market-day stalls
And maison knife slices.

The coffee cup steams red under Euskal Herria,
The cigarette's sibilant whisper as we chug past
Another charred auctioneer's.

Frankfurt Am Main

This winter the hole in my shoe let the cold in
So I travel over Köln mountains
To translate my Deutschmarks to where English is broadly spoken
Mouthing gasoline along the highway.

Kommt du hier, mein shatz
I'm barely covered by your lungi
And reluctantly burn the candle
Of the couple in wax embrace

The pollen dust took my imprint this morning.
Settled with coffee
I drizzle honey over my breakfast under the pecan tree
While the Spanish moss lolls in the persuasive air.

The autumn settles into glühwein
And I lob knoblauch and wurst
Into the turning leaves of a great Magnolia
By whose bole I remain.

Geography

I was shipped home at seven stone on Christmas Eve
And sent to the Ranch
Where last I'd been on Wednesday half-days
For pork chops and gravy.

When the chat turned interesting by hush,
I was hooshed out to the car
Past Dan who spat his Player's No. 6 phlegm into the fire.

Denmark, Copenhagen
The Waal, the Maas, the Lek

The Rhine is the sewer of Europe.

Pagoda

THOMAS MARTIN

Simon leaned against the motorcycle and watched from the track as Tilda knelt on the forest floor. She had her back to him and was carefully adjusting the aperture on her camera. They had stopped so that she could take a photograph of a gigantic tree, a monster whose bark fell over the crumbling wall of an ancient Khmer ruin, its wood split like some leviathan hand pulling the building back into the bush, reclaiming it for the jungle. Simon curved the blade of a Swiss army knife around the edge of a thick aloe vera leaf he was holding, squeezing the sap onto his forearm and rubbing its jelly into his skin. He didn't take his eyes off Tilda.

The rain came suddenly, clapping against the canopy high above them, loud as applause in a packed theatre. It lasted only a few moments but it was startling and made her turn from her photography. She stood up, facing him with a look of wonder, and almost smiled. He was breathless for a second, struck by what a beautiful mess she was, her hair partially stuck to her forehead with sweat, her knees muddy below the hem of her shorts. The jungle affected him, the smell of the trees, the moisture. It stirred him to look at her in it. He picked up the water canister and stepped away from the motor bike, moving from the track onto the thick mulch toward her. Tilda watched carefully as he stopped to shake large drops from a fern and onto his face, wetting his lips.

He handed her the flask, which she took, his fingers lingering over hers. Simon leaned forward as she drank, his head slightly behind hers, his fingers gently touching the inch of exposed skin between her t-shirt and the waist band of her shorts. With a slightly open mouth, he brought his lips down against the nape of her neck. But they burned with the sharp bitter taste of her and he drew back, putting his fingers to his mouth which tingled all over. Tilda had sprayed fresh DEET on to her neck and arms when they had stopped last. The acrid taste of the mosquito repellent left the skin on his lips stinging. She shoved him out of the way and walked stolidly back to the motorcycle.

'Come on, Simon. That rain could have messed the roads. It might be just dirt tracks to the Pagoda for all we know. And the sun will be setting soon. I can't miss that. Do you even know how far away we are?'

'Out here, it feels like we're the only two people left in the world,' he said.

She laughed derisively.

'What a cheap line. You're such a juvenile sometimes. You think you can *fuck* me here on the forest floor and all is forgotten?'

He looked blankly at her. She frowned, raised her camera to her face, and shot him standing there in front of the ruin and the tree.

The drive was fast through the jungle; the path was well worn and relatively dry from the cover of the trees. But the jungle gradually fell away and then it was just a track through miles of watery fields that ran north of Preah Vihear and to the horizon, Laos.

The rain had tinged everything brown. His eyes had to seek out the sporadic patches of green reeds in the rice fields that flanked them for miles. They passed a few huge oxen, bags of skin and bone, wading through sludge, chewing and swatting mosquitoes from their hides with the brushes of their tails. He squinted into the distance, the brown and red colour seemed to evaporate into the sky and his focus blurred for a moment. His scarf was pulled tightly over his nose, flecked with mud. The driving was becoming slow, hard work. He struggled with the motorcycle, shifting his weight to keep them balanced as he weaved around the stagnant ponds of rainwater that were becoming larger as they got farther along the dirt road. It was completely washed over in places, steam rippling off it, submerged rocks sending shudders through the handlebars and into his body. The air was heavy and he couldn't maintain a straight line long enough to build pace and create a breeze. There was an agoraphobic sparseness to the surroundings that made him long for the cover of the rain forest. The wheels turned slow revolutions, flicking streaks of red and brown dirt against their legs.

He felt her arms move around him. She had been holding back until then, carefully clasping the back bar, trying not to touch him, holding her legs out from his body like wings. But now she moved onto him, wrapping him in a backwards embrace, her bare legs slicked with mud, straddling him from behind as her hands moved across the front of his chest and clasped each other, locking over his belly. Her body was warm against his. The sensation of her breath on his neck was intoxicating after the days they had spent apart. Maybe she had forgiven him, he thought, or maybe she was just as achingly tired as he was and was giving in, a tight knot uncoiling. Simon clung to the idea of forgiveness and it urged him on. He managed to build up speed by staying riskily close to the edge of the ditch. Then he caught sight of the hill in the distance.

Everything had become dull, the colours washed out in the rain and he had to strain his eyes to see it. The plan had been to reach the hill and climb to the top where there was a small Pagoda from which they could watch the sun set over the rice fields of northern Cambodia. He had glimpsed it from the corner of his eye. Hypnotized by the horizon, the Pagoda had emerged from the landscape like a secret from one of those trick paintings you have to stare at to see the second image. For a moment the road became the sky. The front wheel turned suddenly in a jack-knife but the bike kept moving forwards, the wheels turning slower than they were travelling, almost gliding on top of the hot muck. The brakes had lost traction. In a second her arms were gone from him, the motorbike vanished from under them and everything was red and brown mud.

He raised his head from the road. Dirty water streamed from his hair, staining his neck and the collar of his shirt. The bike had slid four or five metres in front, the tyre tracks sweeping a wide berthed pattern in the mud. It lay half-submerged in the ditch, the front wheel up and spinning. Simon pushed himself upright. He looked around but couldn't see her. Turning in a circle, he said her name, then shouted it as he ran back along the road, skirting the ditch in a panic. Then he saw an arm and a leg grappling against the edge of the ridge that ran down into the water of a rice field. It was a four-foot drop into the rancid stagnant dyke. Tilda was struggling to hold herself out of it, clutching a root protruding from the side. The water moved with a thick layer of mosquitoes that burst into a cloud as his foot sent a rock in with a splash. His heart skipped when he saw the long sleek body of a snake just under the surface of the liquid. He quickly curled his arm around her waist and rolled her back onto the road. Their bodies lay tangled and panting.

He sat up and held her face. Tilda's eyes opened and she groaned.

'Are you alright?' he asked as he moved his hands carefully over her, checking her bones.

'I'm fine, I think,' she replied, rubbing her head as she pushed herself upright.

'Are you sure?'

'Your eyes are frightened,' she said.

Simon's lip was bleeding. Tilda put her fingers to it and softly smudged the blood around his lips. They both had their hands on each other's faces and she leaned in to kiss him but stopped. Remembering that she was supposed to hate him now, she pulled away and covered her face with her hands and started to cry. Her shoulders heaved under the sobs. Simon reached his hands to hers but she flung them from her face, clenching her own into fists. Her eyes were red, two tears cutting a clean line on her cheek. He fell back deflated and they sat on the muddy road looking at each other.

'I'm sorry,' he said.

'Don't. Just don't. Your apology is hollow.'

'I feel terrible but I can't go back in time. I can't just wash everything away.'

'Your sins you mean? Well maybe you should try bathing in something cleaner, you bastard.' She flung a fistful of dirt at him. It slugged him in the shoulder, his whole body dripped with it anyway.

'So where do we go from here?'

'That's the question isn't it? Do you want to go back, Simon? Do we turn back now?' Her eyes were searching. He knew how loaded her question was, how many directions it moved in. She didn't want to go back. Always move forwards was her philosophy. He looked to the ominous sky. The clouds were so grey and black in places that the sun could have set behind them and night could have arrived without them noticing. If it rained again, the roads would be awash and he wouldn't be able to get them home in the darkness. He wasn't even sure if the bike had survived the crash, or if they had. And there was a storm coming. If the Pagoda wasn't habitable, they were in trouble. But maybe they had gone too far to turn back now. Simon was confused. He closed his eyes and thought of going right back, undoing everything. He imagined the road being sucked back into the wheels, retracting the journey downriver, the smell of the open sewers of Phnom Penh rushing out of their noses, across the border to Vietnam, Saigon again but backwards, conversations of betrayal unspoken, the tides of Munet go in and out in reverse, the phosphorescence dissolves into the water, he pulls himself out of her in the moonlight, the kites in the square at Hué drop from the sky, his beard disappears into a skin that is lightening, an old man takes the Japanese military issue Honda from him and hands him a thousand US dollars, then into the air and down, spit coffee out into a cup at Frankfurt airport, into the air again and moonwalk out through the gates at Heathrow, let go of her hand and swallow the words – *let's stay away for ever.*

'It's your choice. Are you turning back?' she said. 'We can drive to Siem Reap. I can sell the bloody bike. You can go. I can give you money for your ticket home, or wherever. If that's what you want, Simon. Is it?'

He kept his eyes closed and shook his head.

She stood looking into the ditch as he used all his weight to wrestle the bike upright. He kicked the pedal start a few times and it choked and spluttered on. A five-foot cobra floated on the surface of the still water. It had been dead for at least a day. Flies moved back and forth in frenzy over its decaying head.

The sky was getting darker as they pressed on. Simon heard the grumble of thunder in the distance. He flicked the lights which blinked a few times before staying on.

There was a clutch of houses at the base of the hill. Some were no more than huts covered in straw. All stood on high stilts of wood lifted from the flooded fields. They were huddled under the sparse protection of some palm trees whose thick fans of leaves moved in the wind, high above the dwellings. Groups of half-naked children spilled from the gaps and the cracks in the structures and rushed the light of the motorcycle. They repeated 'Halo, Halo' over and over, their small hands reaching out and touching Simon's arm. As the children begged for alms, adults watched from a distance. Simon looked at their homes, wondering how the weak-looking buildings didn't get washed away in the monsoon. Tilda made faces and played with the children who ran about her, their bellies bloated with malnutrition. They laughed and pointed at the two strangers who were almost red as the mud dried and turned to clay against their skin.

Concrete stairs had been built into the side of the hill because it was so steep at the base. He didn't try to help her up the large steps and went ahead, his eyes searching out the path that twisted around the side of the mound in a smile. The higher they climbed, the rockier and muddier it became. A couple of local men with a goat passed them. One stopped and pointed at the sky before making motions of rainfall with his fingers. Simon looked at the man's badly mangled hand.

By the time they were within eyeshot of the Pagoda, large drops of rain were falling periodically. Simon took his rain poncho out of his bag and tossed it to her. She had forgotten hers and offered a half-smile in thanks.

The grey had disappeared from the skyline. There were streaks of black cloud laid like smoke now, upon a sky that seemed suddenly to be a brilliant white. The landscape spread before them, an expanse of green and brown. They watched the flooded rice fields, laid flat like shards of glass, stretch into the horizon, all the way to the snake of the Mekong Delta.

Then the thunder clapped its huge booming presence. The dead heat was about to break, the earth was gasping for it. They made it to the gate of the simple Pagoda just in time and rushed under a small wooden shelter, an observation deck that looked out over the land. Tilda was breathing hard with the exultation of racing the storm. The hood of the poncho had blown back from her face.

There was a plant growing against the side of the shelter. Its flowers were in bloom and the petals fell in tassels over the awning in a thick waterfall of red.

'It's like that plant you used to grow back home in the green-house,' she said, holding up a portion in her hand. 'What was it called again?' He knew she knew the name but was making him say it.

'It looks like an Amaranthus.'

'But the garden name?'

'Love-Lies-Bleeding,' he said, 'but it's South American. I don't think it grows here.'

Simon turned away from her and pulled a handful of the plant aside like a curtain so that they could look across the courtyard to the temple. A boy, no more than seventeen, had appeared in the doorway of the Wat. He had the bald head, the drooping ears and the serene face of a Siddhartha. His skin was a deep golden honey against the bright ochre lungi that was wrapped loosely about his body. The thunder came again, loud and near. Then the sky opened. Its white colour was turning orange and was blood red around the edge of the black storm cloud. Simon looked from the boy to the eerie skyline. It was as if the sun were being smothered rather than setting. The rain got harder and harder, huge and unrelenting.

The young monk stepped out into the blur of the courtyard and walked to the centre. The cloth of his robes slapped tightly against his skin as it soaked up the flood, beads of water rolling off his head. They watched him as he stopped by a small stone stool and placed something on top of it. He opened his hands as if in prayer and raised his face to the onslaught of the water. Then he began to turn slowly, unwrapping his cloth. He let it drop to the ground, revealing a toned youthful body, and picked up the small object from the stone. It was soap. He moved the bar across his nakedness, building a thick white lather on his skin, letting the rain water wash it off.

Simon was engrossed, and then surprised as Tilda grabbed him to her. There was urgency in her fingers as she ripped some of the buttons and tugged opened his shirt, pulling it roughly from his back. She held the ripped garment in her hand and pushed him from the shelter, out towards the monk. The rush of water was suddenly all around Simon, drenching him. Tilda watched as it beat hard against him, a white skin emerging as rivers of red dirt ran off.

Biographies

Gerard Lee has worked as a freelance actor for twenty years, having trained at the Samuel Beckett Centre in Trinity College Dublin. He has published poetry in *The Shop* and in *Poetry Ireland Review*. He has also written for *Sunday Miscellany* on RTÉ, and is included in *Best of Sunday Miscellany 1995-2000*. He is married to Paula, and his two favourite poems are MollyRose (9) and Nancy (6).

Antonia Hart was born in Dublin. She studied law at Trinity College Dublin, and has an MA in Journalism from Dublin City University and an MSc in Multimedia Systems, also from Trinity. Her work has been published in the *Momaya Annual Review* and the *Stinging Fly*. She was twice longlisted for the Fish International Short Story Competition.

Therese Caherty is a journalist working and writing in Dublin.

Craig Caulfield is native of Boston's North Shore. He received a degree from the University of Vermont in 2005, graduating with Honors in English and History. His non-fiction book, *Ruggles Street*, has just gone into its third printing.

Johanna Foster grew up in NYC. She has lived in Austria, Germany and the Netherlands before moving to Dublin.

Anna Murphy grew up in County Tipperary and now lives in County Wicklow. She has worked as a print and radio journalist and is currently a reporter with RTÉ News.

Erik Vatne was raised in Schraalenburgh, New Jersey. He was educated at The Barnstable Academy, Bard College and University College Dublin. His work has appeared or is forthcoming in *Barrow Street*, *The Paris Review*, *The Brooklyn Review*, *The Philadelphia City Paper* (2nd Prize Annual Poetry Contest) and *The Allegheny Review*.

Jonathan Cooper was born in Wolverhampton in 1981, and studied English at the University of York. He has written plays workshopped at *The Door*, the Birmingham REP's new writing space, and has had a series of monologues, *'Parentheses'*, performed at The King's Head theatre in Islington. He is currently working on a novel.

Ragnar Almqvist was born in Dublin in 1983. He graduated from University College Dublin in November 2005, with a degree in German and English. In addition to literature, he takes a keen interest in politics, psychology and education theory. He intends to pursue studies in education theory when he finishes at Trinity in September.

Jennifer Brady has had stories published in the *Stinging Fly* magazine and *Southword Journal*. She was shortlisted for the Sean O'Faolain Short Story Competition 2003 and specially selected for *'Short Short'* Story Competition by Dave Eggers in The *Guardian* in 2004. She has written and directed a one-act monologue, which was performed in Players Theatre, TCD as part of New Writers' Week 2006.

Luke Anderson lives in Charlottesville, Virginia, at the foot of the Blue Ridge Mountains. He received a degree in English literature from the University of Virginia in 2005, and is currently seeking publication for his first novel.

Megan Paslawski was born in Philadelphia and raised in New England. She studied English Literature and Political Science at McGill University in Montreal, which she now considers her hometown. This summer, she will be the 2006 Writing Director for the New England Playwrights Project. Her work appears in the spring edition of *Southword Journal*.

Keith Payne travelled for seven years before attending Trinity College, Dublin, where he read English. He is currently working on a collection of poetry.

Thomas Martin graduated from University College Dublin with a first-class honours degree in English and Philosophy. He won the UCD literary society's short story of the year 2005, has published short stories in *The Sunday Tribune* and has twice been short-listed for the Hennessy New Irish Writing award.

Contact details for these writers are available at www.tcd.ie/OWC and www.incorrigiblyplural.com